"The domestic violence issue is more universal than is currently recognized. This handbook challenges and equips pastors and ministry leaders to reflect and engage in practical solutions to domestic violence existing in our faith communities. Murphy's field experience and academic rigor lends a solid foundation to this work."

The Rev. Aubrey Gregory
Senior Pastor, Newark Gospel Tabernacle
Newark, New Jersey

"Nancy Murphy has produced an important handbook that will prove inestimable to pastors. This is a subject that no pastor or Christian leader can or should avoid. All of us are either part of the problem or part of the solution. By God's grace, I want to be part of the solution!"

W. Ward Gasque, Ph.D.
President, Pacific Association of Theological Studies
Seattle, Washington

"The prophets of old called God's people to see the tears of the oppressed, bind up the brokenhearted and loose the chains of injustice. Today, modern-day prophets like Nancy Murphy continue the clarion call for justice and mercy by waking us up to the tragedy of domestic violence. For far too long the church has either ignored or sadly, even fostered the problem. This helpful handbook helps us pastors open our eyes to the issue and know how we can help. May we all join the growing ranks of those saying, 'No more!'"

The Rev. Jeff Horton
Pastor, Shoreline Free Methodist Church
Shoreline, Washington

"Nancy Murphy has a passion to follow the mandate of Christ in seeking to 'proclaim release to the captives....and free those who are downtrodden.' When she speaks about domestic violence, her voice rings with courage and deep empathy. We must listen to what she has to declare to the Church on this issue."

The Rev. Denny Gunderson
Pastor, Author, Therapist,
Domestic Violence Intervention Specialist

God's Reconciling Love:

A Pastor's Handbook on Domestic Violence

Nancy A. Murphy, M.A.

With contributions from:
Cindy S. Bohnett, The Rev. Dr. Randy J. Bridges, The Rev. Dr. Luis A. Carlo,
The Rev. Keith Galbraith, Karla S. McElroy, The Rev. Nathaniel J. Mullen, Gail J. Mullen,
Judge David A. Steiner

Foreword by Dr. Dan B. Allender

Working together to end
sexual & domestic violence

2400 N 45th St. Suite 10
Seattle, WA 98103
www.faithtrustinstitute.org

God's Reconciling Love: A Pastor's Handbook on Domestic Violence

Nancy A. Murphy, M.A.

With contributions from:
Cindy S. Bohnett, The Rev. Dr. Randy J. Bridges, The Rev. Dr. Luis A. Carlo,
The Rev. Keith Galbraith, Karla S. McElroy, The Rev. Nathaniel J. Mullen,
Gail J. Mullen, Judge David A. Steiner

Foreword by Dr. Dan B. Allender

FaithTrust
INSTITUTE
Working together to end
sexual & domestic violence

FaithTrust Institute
2400 N. 45th Street, Suite 10
Seattle, WA 98103
www.faithtrustinstitute.org

All Scripture quotations are taken from the HOLY BIBLE, NEW
INTERNATIONAL VERSION. Copyright © 1973, 1978, 1984 International
Bible Society. Used by permission of Zondervan Bible Publishers.

Cover photograph by Cara Chandler

Design by Lomax design

ISBN 0-9745189-0-5

Printed in the United States of America

Acknowledgments

I would like to extend my gratitude to Jean Anton of FaithTrust Institute for mentoring me through this project. Her patience was endless.

Work of this nature requires many contributors, and I would like to sincerely thank writers Cindy S. Bohnett, The Rev. Dr. Randy J. Bridges, Vivian Burnett, The Rev. Dr. Luis A. Carlo, The Rev. Keith Galbraith, Dr. Catherine Clark Kroeger, Karla S. McElroy, Dr. Nancy Nason-Clark, The Rev. Nathaniel J. and Mrs. Gail J. Mullen, Dee Myers, Linda Paz, Judge David A. Steiner and Candie Warren for their candid and thoughtful contributions. Not all written contributions are included in this work, yet they served to guide it. Thank you.

To Heidi Symington, Jen Crum, Maxine Covington, Thomas B. Murphy, Joy Pardo, the Board and Staff of Northwest Family Life, and the Esther Network, I wish to pay a special tribute for their meaningful support, both of me personally and of the critical work to end domestic violence.

This handbook is dedicated to The Rev. Richard and Mrs. Patricia Parlee, The Rev. Ed and Mrs. Ollie Alexander and The Rev. Earle and Mrs. Louise Johnson for leading the way in providing safety, accountability and reconciliation.

Thank you.

Foreword

I stood absent-mindedly waiting to check out of our local grocery store. I was thinking of picking up a copy of *The Star*, a brazen journalistic rendition of alien visits, celebrity pregnancies related to Elvis, and a potpourri of other bizarre stories. I thought better of it, but just as I turned away from the rack I heard a couple arguing just a few people in front of me. Apparently, the wife had forgotten her checkbook and he didn't have his wallet. The normal noise of check out lanes quieted in an instant and intensified the hiss of his voice as he spoke in harsh, restrained terms. "I told you never to shop without first checking to see if you have your checkbook." She looked down at the floor. Her withdrawal only seemed to intensify his fury. He grabbed her purse and began to rummage around. He swore. She apologized and he shoved it back into her arms. Then he stormed out, leaving her with the groceries and the unpaid bill.

I wondered what would happen on the ride home, or once they arrived home. Would he need a few drinks before he hit her? Or was the pattern set to such a feverous pitch that he would jerk her arm even as they walked to the car and then drive home treacherously, intending to push her even further into a state of terror?

I was a witness to the first round of an escalating story of abuse. I don't think what I saw was the first, nor will it be the last encounter of harm she will face. And all I did was stare at them with the same bewilderment that I felt as I looked at the bizarre newspaper.

They were an anomaly. Thoughtful and decent people don't buy *The Star*. Good, middle-class men don't hurt their wives. I stared at both the couple and newspaper as aliens to my comfortable and well-ordered world.

But I am wrong. People in an upscale neighborhood do buy *The Star*. And middle class, upper class, and lower socio-economic class men do hurt their wives and girlfriends. There is an increasing rise in violence in our grocery stores, neighborhoods, churches, and homes. We can't remain silent, bewildered, or numb.

A prominent Rabbi, when asked if there is any lesson to be learned from the Holocaust, answered, "No more perpetrators. No more victims. No more bystanders. No more silence." His cry speaks to us all. We all fit into one of those three categories, and the vast majority of us have assumed that domestic violence is someone else's problem, that it is not an issue in our family, in our community. That is a lie.

I too have spoken abusive words to my wife. It grieves me to say she has seen fury in my eyes when I felt shame due to something she had said or done. I may not have responded to the degree that constitutes domestic abuse, but I have sinned against my wife with the anger that Jesus calls murder (Matthew 5:21-28).

And too often, in countless settings, I've seen the tip of the iceberg of abuse and turned my eyes away. I've assumed it was not right for me to intervene, that it was none of my business.

It *is* my business, just as it was the business of the loving Samaritan to get involved in aiding the bruised and beaten man assaulted by robbers. The question I hear countless good-hearted pastors and laypeople ask is "What can I do? I know violence exists, and I fear it happens even in my own congregation, but other than pray and suffer for those who experience an assault, what can I really do that won't add more shame or harm to the victim?"

This well-designed manual, written and compiled by Nancy Murphy, a wise and amazing woman, will not only answer the majority of your core questions, but will embolden you to make the path safe for both victim and perpetrator. Nancy's words are joined by several other voices from the church community; pastors and laypeople alike add their wisdom and experience to encourage you on your journey.

I am thrilled you are joining us in this labor. The pain of dealing with abuse is immense, yet the honor of doing so is greater. Nothing brings the heart more joy than living out the gospel in the midst of darkness. I pray your awakening to the violence around us draws your heart to the wonder of how God longs to protect the orphan, the widow, and the stranger. May He bless your courage.

Dan B. Allender, Ph.D.
President, Mars Hill Graduate School

Table of Contents

What Does the Lord Require of Us?

To *act justly*~ as Christians we have the responsibility to respond on behalf of the oppressed.

To *love mercy*~ as Christians we are uniquely poised to provide protection for the abused and hope for change for the abuser.

To *walk humbly with our God*~ as Christians we walk with Him and care for His children as He has cared for us.
Micah 6:8

Innumerable deaths, suicides and "accidents" take the physical lives of women, children, men, family members, police officers and friends as the result of domestic violence. Emotional despair and spiritual disillusionment cripple myriad more lives.

For too long, we who believe in salvation have wanted to think that domestic violence happens only outside our sacred communities, in other people's churches or in the homes of the unsaved. Unfortunately, both research and experience have proven us wrong. We can no longer ignore the reality that the frequency of abuse in our homes is no less than in the general population. We are presented with the challenge and the opportunity to use our unique resources and strengths as Christians to bring healing and restoration to hurting families, and to work together to ensure safety for all.

The Church has long served all family members through every stage of life, in celebration and in suffering. Pastors and those of us involved in a ministry capacity have long been sought out as trusted confidantes. Often, we are the first to become aware of the deepest problems a family is facing.

The Church is a community of instruction, of safety, and of love. It is the ideal setting for disclosure and healing. It is one of the only places where the entire family can grow in a healthy relationship with God and with each other.

The wisdom of the Scriptures, the counsel of the Holy Spirit, the love of Christ and the way we demonstrate that love make the difference between life and death. We are a part of the solution to bringing peace to the family.

I pray that, as we awaken to the deepest pain of some of those among us, our homes and our churches will be places where abundant life, not death, is experienced.

In Jesus' name,
Nancy Murphy

Chapter One

An Overview of Domestic Violence

*Don't you know that you yourselves are
God's temple and that God's Spirit lives in
you? If anyone destroys God's temple, God
will destroy him; for God's temple is sacred,
and you are that temple.*

I Corinthians 3:16-17

What is Domestic Violence?

Do•mes•tic: of or relating to the family or household.

Vi•o•lence: 1. Physical force exerted for the purpose of violating, damaging, or abusing. 2. Abusive or unjust exercise of power.

You can *see* violence in a slap or a punch.
You can *hear* violence in a tone of voice, a choice of words.
You can *feel* violence when you witness an act of aggression.
You can *taste* the impact of violence in bitter disappointment, fear and shame.

Under the law[1], domestic violence is the term used for *actual or threatened* physical harm, injury, or assault, sexual assault, or stalking directed against family or household members. In the counselor's view, domestic violence is a recurrent pattern of assaultive and coercive behaviors, or the credible threat of force used to ridicule, humiliate, and gain and maintain power and control over an

[1] Revised Code of Washington: RCW 26.50.010(1),(2),(3)

intimate partner. From a Biblical perspective, any form of abuse is an offense against the Creator and against the image of God reflected in all people.

Domestic violence is a leading cause of injury and death to women worldwide. One in five women around the globe is physically or sexually abused in her lifetime. Gender violence causes more death and disability among women aged 15 to 44 than cancer, malaria, traffic accidents or war.[2] Because 90-95% of domestic violence is committed by men against women and children,[3] we will refer to abusers as "he" and victims as "she" for the purposes of this discussion. We ask the reader to bear in mind that in a small percentage of cases, the abusers are female.

The voice of the church promotes, strengthens, and nurtures family relationships. As we work toward respectful and honoring relationships in marriage and in our families, domestic violence must be addressed. Our theology must be clear that violence is not acceptable in any home. Our responses must be those of mercy, justice and humility. False assumptions and prevailing social norms about domestic violence must be examined and challenged. We must be willing to open the eyes of our hearts to see the truth about domestic violence and abuse.

What Domestic Violence is Not

Six popular myths perpetuate the high prevalence of domestic violence and abuse around the world. These myths must be uncovered and discarded in order for the truth to be known.

Myth 1: Domestic violence is a private matter.

Violence by a spouse or other intimate partner has most often been viewed as a private matter. This is simply untrue. When a woman loses her life at the hands of a trusted loved one, it is everyone's business. The home should be a safe place to grow and be nurtured. The violence and assault that takes place

> "When I was pregnant with my oldest daughter, he started questioning me about an old boyfriend...He didn't like my answers and began slapping me in the face. I was devastated and couldn't believe he was treating me like this...it shocked me. I was deeply hurt and so I tried harder to please him, thinking this would make things better. It never did."
>
> Debbie, Church of Christ

---

[2] Kroeger, Catherine Clark and Nancy Nason-Clark, *No Place for Abuse: Biblical & Practical Resources to Counteract Domestic Violence.* Downer's Grove, IL: IVP, 2001 (Back Cover)

[3] *Bureau of Justice Statistics Selected Findings: Violence Between Intimates* (NCJ-149259). November 1994.

within intimate relationships should rally an even greater public outrage than assault by a stranger. Other family members, friends, bystanders can be caught in the crossfire of domestic violence. The societal costs from domestic violence are staggering to our educational systems, our legal systems, our health systems, our criminal justice systems, our neighborhoods, our workplaces and our congregations.

Particularly vulnerable are the future generations. Children who witness abuse have ringside seats. Even when they are not directly abused themselves, they are ten times more likely to become the next generation of abusers or victims.[4] They are six times more likely to commit suicide, twenty-four times more likely to commit a sexual assault, 50% more likely to abuse drugs and alcohol, and 74% more likely to commit crimes against others.[5] Clearly the violence that these children witness radiates outward to society, and down through the generations. *Domestic violence is not a private matter.*

Myth 2: Women provoke the violence.

Another false assumption is that battered women provoke their abuse. The abuser bears sole responsibility for his actions. There is no behavior on the part of the victim that causes or excuses abuse. Offenders often attempt to falsely accuse and disgrace their victims in order to shift blame away from them. It is important to remember that, even in those cases where the victim has violated the marriage in some way, violence is never a legitimate response. The abuser has other avenues of appropriate response available – to seek outside help, or to leave the situation. Violence is *never* an appropriate response. *Women do not provoke the violence.*

Myth 3: Alcohol and drugs "cause" domestic violence.

It is a popular misconception that alcohol and drug use "causes" domestic violence, and that the elimination of the substance abuse problem will eliminate the problem of violence. While it is true that drug and alcohol use often co-occurs with domestic violence, many studies have revealed that alcohol and drugs do not cause violence in the home.[6,7] Clearly the frequency of violent incidents and severity of injury may be increased under the influence, but neither alcohol nor

[4] Jaffe et al. 1986: cf. Statistics Canada 1993

[5] Moore, Sheila Y. 1999. "Adolescent Boys Are the Underserved Victims of Domestic Violence." *Boston Globe,* December 26, p. E7

[6] Sonkin D., Martin D. and Walker L.E., *The Male Batterer: A Treatment Approach.* New York: Springer, 1985

[7] Walker L. *The Battered Woman Syndrome.* New York: Springer, 1984.

drugs is at the root of the violence. Rather, the desire for power and control over another person is at the root of the violence. Not all batterers drink or abuse drugs, nor do all those who drink or abuse drugs batter. When substance abuse and violence co-occur, each must be addressed separately. *The desire for power and control over others, not alcohol and drug use, is the root cause of domestic violence.*

Myth 4: Violence simply "erupts" suddenly out of nowhere.

Domestic violence and abuse is *not* about sudden loss of control. On the contrary, it is a systematic pattern of behavior used to control a loved one. Sometimes violence grows out of immediate anger, but in many other instances, batterers are very calm and intentional about their abuse. Often, what may have begun as a subtle form of abuse grows over a period of time into more overt violence. Left unchecked, frequency and intensity can escalate, even to the point of ending in murder and/or suicide. *Domestic violence is a systematic pattern of abusive behavior that develops and escalates over time.*

Myth 5: Violence and abuse are always physical.

Usually we think of domestic violence in terms of physical or sexual abuse. But abuse takes many forms. Most clearly defined are physical, verbal, sexual, spiritual, emotional, economic, social, and psychological abuse. These frequently coexist and produce a pattern of relationship in which the perpetrator's behavior intimidates the victim and cuts her off from healthy relationships in family, church,

"After 43 years of an abusive marriage, she was only 'allowed' to go to the grocery store on Thursdays between 9:00 and 10:00. Basically she became my father's prisoner in her own home."

Cynthia, Baptist

and workplace; robs her of the financial independence to change her circumstances; saps her sense of self-worth and self-determination; and leaves her in constant fear for her safety and that of her children. Many victims of domestic violence become so isolated and ashamed that they begin to believe that *they* are the problem, somehow deserving the abuse they receive. They become desensitized to their emotions and hopeless for change. *Violence and abuse take many forms and can be measured by their destructive effects on the well-being of the victim.*

Myth 6: Abusive men cannot change.

Certainly abusive men can change. God changes hearts. But, changed behavior does not occur overnight or simply because one is sorry. Change begins with surrender. The abuser must admit that he has a problem. Unfortunately, many abusers are unwilling to admit this. These men remain dangerous and will not change as long as they refuse to take responsibility for their behavior. Those who acknowledge their problem and seek help must demonstrate a commitment to be accountable. *Abusive men can change. Real change requires time and hard work.*

The Historical Response to Domestic Violence [8]

Until the 1980s, there were few laws to protect women and children from violence and abuse. Sadly, our churches were committed to keeping the families together at all costs, silently standing by as women suffered in anguish.

Encouraging compliance

Early domestic violence intervention encouraged the victim to be more compliant in the belief that if she were more submissive, she would not provoke the violence. *She was identified as the cause of the violence.* Women were prescribed medications for depression and anxiety, symptoms commonly found among victims of violence and abuse. This approach assumed that if she would just do something different, he would change. Significantly, women who tried to become more submissive often found that it had the opposite effect. Interpersonal violence escalated. Confused, they began to speak out about their abuse. Assertiveness, too, often increased their risk of violence. Counseling became the natural next step as women attempted to break the silence.

Family or Marital Counseling

The next intervention to gain popularity was family or marital therapy for issues such as co-dependency, communication and conflict resolution. The underlying assumption was that if the victim would stop enabling the abuser's behavior, or if they could learn to talk things over, then the conflicts would be resolved and fewer violent episodes would result. *Problems in the relationship were identified as the cause of the violence.* This, too, has turned out to be a faulty assumption. In reali-

---

[8] Adapted from Doug Bartholomew's "Domestic Violence Perpetrator Counselor Training." Kirkland, WA. April 1995.

ty, a victim of abuse who confides in a counselor or pastor faces escalating violence at home as her abuser feels humiliated and exposed. Domestic violence may well be indicative of a problem in a family, but the use of violence or abuse is strictly an individual problem. It is a problem in the abuser, and must be addressed as such if the violence is to end.

Anger Management

The next intervention, still in use, is anger management. The individual with the problem is sent for help – alone, without his partner. The simple assumption is if he can just manage his anger, he won't lose control and hurt others. *Uncontrolled anger was identified as the cause of domestic violence.* While this represented a move in the right direction, it soon became apparent that not all batterers use anger to control their victims. Conversely, not all men who have trouble with anger are batterers. Research shows that there are at least two kinds of batterers – those whose emotions quickly boil over, and those who are cool and methodical as they inflict pain and humiliation on their partners without expressing any angry emotions at all.[9] Other research suggests that some batterers have serious mental illnesses, in addition to problems with power and control, which underlie their use of violence.[10] For still others, battering is a behavior learned as they witnessed abuse in their childhood homes. Thus, anger management programs alone are not an adequate response to domestic violence.

Arrest Laws

Mandatory arrest laws have been introduced in many states for those who physically assault, threaten, or stalk an intimate partner. While the abuser is taken to jail, the victim is provided with referrals to shelters and services designed to provide advocacy for her and for her children. *For the first time, the abuser himself was seen as the cause of the domestic violence.* Those who care about "image" are willing to get help. Consequently, many working in the field believe that arrest and incarceration for domestic violence is the most successful technique for getting violent men to stop abusing. An important caution: In some cases, arrest can increase physical violence, particularly when the men do not have good community ties or a need to conform to social pressures.

---

[9]Dutton, Donald G, PhD and Susan K. Goland. *The Batterer: A Psychological Profile.* New York: Basic Books, 1997.

[10] Jacobson, Neil S. and John M. Gottman. *When Men Batter Women: New Insights into Ending Abusive Relationships.* New York: Simon & Schuster Adult Publishing Group, 1998.

Domestic Violence Treatment Programs

In North America, a new counseling model to stop violence in the home has developed. Judges in the criminal justice system can order a batterer to attend approved counseling sessions. State laws detail the requirements for a Domestic Violence Intervention Program. Men entering these programs are required to attend weekly single-gender groups for a specified period of time (in Washington state, a minimum of a year), or they go back to jail for their crime. For first-time misdemeanor offenses, satisfactory completion of treatment will expunge the charge from the record.

Coordinated Community Response

The most effective strategy in intervening in the cycle of violence is known as a Coordinated Community Response. Coming together around this issue in order to address it with a unified voice are the legal system, advocacy groups, treatment providers, health care providers, religious communities, local governments, and educational institutions. As we come to an agreement on the definitions of violence and strategize our responses, we keep victim safety as our top priority. When we speak with a collective voice, our message will be neither fragmented nor contradictory, but a unified community call to stop domestic violence.

The Church and Domestic Violence

With the law taking this problem seriously, many abusers begin to rethink their roles, rights and responsibilities within the relationship. This is an opportunity for the Church to bring God into the equation. Without polarizing regarding the roles of men and women, headship, chain of command, and submission, we can agree that God is close to the brokenhearted. This includes *all* members of a family touched by violence. Men who abuse are clearly full of shame and fear. Women and children who are abused are trapped, isolated, ashamed, and hopeless.

Calling on the Great Healer, the Church can bring mercy to the offender by extending God's grace and love, justice to the victim by introducing accountability into the family relationships, and reconciliation of relationships where possible. Certainly individual reconciliation of each family member to Jesus Christ is the highest goal. The reconciling love of God is a gift of enormous magnitude.

> *God made him who had no sin to be sin*
> *for us, so that in him we might become the*
> *righteousness of God.*
> 2 Corinthians 5:21
> Why? So we can be reconciled to God. This is
> always possible. *God is love…*
> 1 John 4:16
> *Who shall separate us from the love of Christ?*
> Romans 8:35

Sadly, it is not always possible for our human relationships to be fully reconciled. Violence breaks the vows to love, honor and cherish, and there is hope for restoration only if the abuser stops abusing.[11] A lack of repentance makes it unwise to work toward the reconciliation of relationship. Many women around the world have lost their lives at the hands of their husbands, when reconciliation without repentance was attempted.

Domestic violence is a crime under the law. In the eyes of God it is a sin, committed by a perpetrator, as is murder, adultery, lying, cheating, etc. The stigma of the names "perpetrator," "abuser," "offender," "sinner" is overwhelming. Yet we understand from the scriptures that not one of us is free from sin, not one of us "good enough." It is only through the work of the cross that there is redemption. "While we were yet sinners, Christ died for us." (Romans 5:6) Those who perpetrate violence in intimate relationships are committing sin at the expense of someone who has loved and trusted them. The church should be a safe place for the sinner to confess, repent, and turn away from sin, and to receive the gift of God's love. However, there is no permission given in the scriptures to continue in our sin, and so the abuser must also be accountable.

The call to the church is, with humility, to study, to pray, to listen, and to learn God's heart for healthy families, and then to come alongside the suffering and facilitate healing for all family members. The abuser must stop the abuse. The ones who are abused must be protected from further injuries and their safety – physically, emotionally, spiritually and financially – must be ensured. They must be given the time needed to heal, for their journey has been grim and painful. Profound sadness and loss must be grieved significantly by all parties.

Healing can take a long time. Only then will it be clear if the relationship can be reconciled. If so, it will take on a completely different form, with newly developed patterns of honor and respect for each other. If not, the one who has been abused must be freed to pursue life in Christ apart from her abuser. For, "The righteous cry out, and the Lord hears them; he delivers them from all their troubles. The Lord is close to the brokenhearted and saves those who are crushed in spirit." (Psalm 34:17-18)

[11] Adapted from Marie Fortune, *Keeping the Faith*. New York: Harper San Francisco, 1987, p. 97.

Chapter Two

Pastors' Perspectives

*It was he who gave some to be apostles,
some to be prophets, some to be evangelists,
and some to be pastors and teachers, to prepare God's people for works of service, so
that the body of Christ may be built up
until we all reach unity in the faith and in
the knowledge of the Son of God and
become mature, attaining to the whole
measure of the fullness of Christ.*
Ephesians 4:11-13

Recently, I heard a young pastor express his angst at the weight of responsibility he feels for the healing process of those in his congregation. He was apologetic, but said he felt that the topic of domestic violence was just one more thing on his plate that threatened to overwhelm him. In order to stay positive, he said, he needed to focus on more fruitful spiritual activities such as worship, contemplative prayer, and preaching.

His point is well taken. Pastors perhaps feel more responsibility for people than any other person of "power." It is crucial that pastors and those with gifts of mercy and service protect themselves from burnout, cynicism, depression, and exhaustion. The trauma that is experienced by families impacted by domestic violence is so significant that those of us who draw near to them can also be traumatized.

Still, there is much that pastors can do to walk with those in pain while depending on the Lord to protect their own well-being and ability to minister to the larger body. Research shows that more abuse victims, abusers, and family members go to church leaders for help than all other helping professionals combined.[12] More perpetrators complete treatment programs when referred by their churches.[13] Thus, pastors who become educated about the dynamics of domestic violence, who offer a scripturally-based theology that denies permission to abuse, who hear and support victims, who hold abusers accountable, and who learn about community resources for referral and assistance can not only reduce trauma, but save lives.

This chapter gives first-person accounts of the perspectives of three ministers. These are the voices of ordinary men who have been called to attend to the extraordinary work of caring for victims and abusers alike. They have learned, as circumstances have presented themselves, how to advocate for victim safety, how to call abusers to account, and how to wait upon the Lord for guidance in reconciliation. No single pastor's account alone can serve as a model, but these stories are offered as examples of one pastor's experience, one pastor's theological reflection, and one pastor's response to the issue of domestic violence.

---

[12] Horton, Anne L. and Judith A. Williamson, *Abuse and Religion: When Praying Isn't Enough.* Lexington, MA: Lexington, 1998, Preface.

[13] Nason-Clark, Nancy and Nancy Murphy, *Celebrating the Graduates: An Exploration into the Nature and Extent of Change in the Lives of Men Who Have Graduated from a Batterers Program.* Paper presented to Northwest Family Life Board of Directors, Seattle, WA: 2003.

A Pastor's Experience

The Rev. Nathaniel J. Mullen is an urban pastor, serving for 21 years. He has been married for 36 years and has three children and two grandchildren.

Pastor Mullen witnessed an episode of domestic violence and was forced on the spot to respond. Since that time, he has been proactive in addressing this issue from the pulpit and in pastoral counseling. He is engaged in a search for root causes, openly shares his observations, looks to the scriptures for guidance, and is clear about what he can and cannot do.

Pastor Mullen has intentionally become educated about the dynamics of domestic violence. In partnership with his wife, Gail, he has been able to provide education to victims of violence who are a part of his community and his congregation and refer them to sources of safety and healing. He supports and respects the choices of battered women.

"Where My Sidewalk Ends"
By The Rev. Nathaniel J. Mullen

In my 30-plus years in the ministry, I have become a student of culture. And what I have observed is that Christian couples and families mirror the prevailing culture. This means that sadly, abuse is found in the church as much as it is in the culture. Most pastors are on the first line of defense for troubled people in the church and the community.

When abuse happens in a church, it is too many times hidden by the abused and the abuser out of fear of rejection by the church congregants. The pews of our churches are littered with the debris of these broken lives. These people sing in our choirs, teach in our Sunday schools, and even fill our pulpits. It is a tragedy that we often pretend these problems don't exist in our sanctuaries. We promote the myth that true believers with real faith don't have these kinds of problems.

We pray for the abused, expecting instantaneous eradication of the problems that took a lifetime to accumulate. I believe in the power of prayer, but healing of emotional, psychological, and physical violation comes not only through prayer but also through being embraced by people of faith with unconditional love. One of the greatest gifts the community of faith can offer is the gift of affirmation.

Over the years, I have developed sensitivity to the hurting and the abused. I remember clearly the day I first discovered the reality of abuse in the congregation. I was pastoring at my first church when violence erupted at a Mother's Day service. It was a perfect spring day. The big stained glass windows were vented open and the fresh scents of spring filled the church with life as the sunlight streamed in. The choir was singing with joy.

After my sermon, it was time for the call to discipleship. I called those who wanted to leave behind a lifestyle of worldliness and bondage to join the ranks of the redeemed to accept the embrace of a loving savior. A tall, attractive woman stepped forward, tugging at the diamond-studded gold band on her finger. She balled her fist up into the hand signal of a people's revolt and thrust the ring at her husband's feet, declaring that she wanted to be free from his ongoing abuse. Without a thought, the husband struck her with such force that the impact cracked the oak pew where she fell. The deacons of the church subdued this man, and the police were called. The shock of this event changed me forever, giving me the resolve to never allow anyone in my congregation to suffer under such abuse, and at the same time somehow to find help for the abuser.

Since that time, I have seen many other horrible examples of abuse. I once confronted a man in my congregation who, I had learned, tortured his wife by burning her with a steam iron if she did not perform her "wifely duties." When the wife showed me her fresh and healed-over scar tissue, I told her I understood her decision to separate from him and would support her whether she reconciled with him or decided to divorce. The stunning fact was that this man felt that he was within his rights to rape and torture his wife because she was his possession. But many times abuse takes more subtle forms. Abuse is any treatment that strips the abused of her humanity and makes her a commodity. Unfortunately, it has been common to think of "wife" as a personal house servant, even using the Bible to defend this position. People who feel damaged or hurt will damage and hurt other people if they don't get the help they need to resolve their personal pain and history. Their pain tends to spill over into the lives of those they interact with.

The Bible sheds light on the equality of male and female, and what it means to be a wife and a husband. Genesis 2:18 tells us "It is not good that man should be alone; I will make a helper *comparable to him*." This verse reveals that mankind has a deep need not only for interaction with his divine creator, but also interaction with his equal. The Bible defines a wife as an equal partner, comparable to man in every way. The purpose of a wife is completion. When this definition is distorted, a wife is placed in an inferior role, and abuse is the common result.

My quest to find help for the victims of abuse has at times been overwhelming. Many of the victims in abuse situations require intensive counseling and support programs. I knew I didn't have enough knowledge to handle it myself. I had to admit the limitations of my training and skill.

The dilemma I found myself in reminds me of the title of the poem I used to read to my first-born son, "Where the Sidewalk Ends." My sidewalk ends when it comes to being able to provide direct counseling and support. Knowing this, I set out to find resources that could help take abused parishioners to the next level of recovery and growth through partnerships with Christian and community agencies that specialized in abuse and recovery. The value of these partnerships cannot be overstated; they make possible the weaving of safety nets for those who have been forced off the edge by violence and abuse.

A Pastor's Reflection

The Rev. Dr. Luis A. Carlo was a first responder to scenes of domestic violence during his 27-year career as a paramedic with the NY Fire Department, Bureau of Emergency Service. Since receiving his Ph.D. from Columbia University, he has addressed issues of domestic violence from his pulpit in the Bronx, at national Christian conferences, in the classrooms of the seminaries where he teaches, and through his work as a board member for The Global Institute on Violence & Exploitation (GIVE). Dr. Carlo proposes *justice* instead of *passivity* as the corrective for violence. His reflection included here (excerpted from a longer article) illustrates how crucial it is that we think theologically about the issue of domestic violence.

"A Theological Reflection on Domestic Violence" By The Rev. Dr. Luis A. Carlo

Of the many biblical themes that are applicable to the problem of domestic violence, we will consider the concepts of *life, peace, and justice*. These themes cut across denominational lines and transcend individual constructs of philosophy and ideology to touch the core of human existence and dignity. We will thus look at life, peace, and justice from a biblical perspective as they relate to domestic violence.

Life and Peace in Creation

The creation accounts in Genesis 1 and 2 tell of God's purpose for humanity. In the beginning the earth was formless and void, darkness was over the surface of the deep. Existence was chaos, confusion, and disorder. God undoes chaos by giving the earth form, fullness, and life, shaping and filling the earth as a dwelling place for humans – male and female – created in the image of God. Design, harmony, order, and life have come forth out of chaos, confusion, and disorder. The peace of God is in all of creation.

But what is peace? In Hebrew, peace is *shalom* – not simply the absence of conflict, but the presence of *wholeness, integrity, and completeness*. Man and woman lived in total harmony with God, self, and each other, and they manifested the design and handiwork of God in their lives. Ellison[14] names eight essential

14 Ellison, Craig W. *From Stress to Well-Being.* Waco, TX: Word Publishing, Inc., 1994, pp. 12-15.

qualities of *shalom* that were intrinsic in man and woman at creation: genuine acceptance, belonging, competence, equity, identity, security, significance, and transcendence. Man and woman were united and interdependent, sharing a positive life of absolute fulfillment in relationship with God.[15]

The Fall and Violence

In Genesis 3 we read that man and woman willfully disregarded God's decree and ate fruit from the forbidden tree, bringing judgment upon themselves. Peace was shattered and chaos was reintroduced into creation. The world and humanity were fractured by conflict and pain. The eight qualities of *shalom* were distorted. After the fall, acceptance is met with rejection and shame; belonging with isolation; competence with inadequacy; equity with victimization; identity with confusion; security with anxiety; significance with worthlessness; and transcendence with anomie, meaninglessness, and chaos.[16] Man and woman were alienated from God. They were filled with shame, guilt, and fear. They experienced conflict in their relationship with each other and a dishonoring community grew out of this conflict.

The first act of violence after the fall (Genesis 4) was fratricide, when Cain killed his brother Abel. God did not return violence for violence, but nevertheless, God's judgment was swift. Cain was sent away from God's presence to become a restless wanderer. When he realized that he would be forever accountable for his action, Cain would have preferred death; but God spared him and Cain carried the consequences with him for the rest of his life. God's answer for death was life and for violence, justice. But because life and peace is what God ordained for all of creation from the beginning, God is still moving creation in that direction. Through justice, God continues to work for peace.

Relational theologian Marjorie Hewitt Suchocki describes original sin as "the fall to violence."[17] The sin of violence is the distorted human personality seeking to survive through aggression. Suchocki states: "Killing is violence; greed and verbal abuse are also violence. Violence has many forms existing along a continuum from obvious to subtle, but at its base, violence is the destruction of well-being."[18] Well-

---

[15] Ibid., p.11.
[16] Ibid., pp. 19-23.
[17] Hewitt Suchocki, Marjorie. *The Fall to Violence: Original Sin and Relational Theology.* New York: Continuum, 1995. See Chapter 5, "Sin Through Violence."
[18] Ibid., p. 85

being, peace, wholeness, integrity, harmony, and completeness is what God intended for all of creation from the beginning. If this is so, then how should the church respond to violence? The corrective for violence is not simply non-violence; it is justice.

Justice: A Response to Violence

We live in a world where there is oppression, genocide, rape, apartheid, torture, human trafficking, and myriad forms of violence that destroy God's peace. All through human history, God has been working to reestablish the peace, the shalom, the well-being of creation. This ministry is also given to the church (Jeremiah 29:7). Peace is not just the absence of tension. It is also the presence of justice. *The path to peace was and continues to be justice.*

It is the Christian's responsibility to unite with God's purpose of reestablishing peace and order. Salvation, therefore, cannot simply be a self-centered survival from ultimate judgment; it must also include the reconciliation of God's whole world to God's established purposes. The entire creation waits to be liberated from its bondage to decay (Romans 8:18-22). How, then, are believers to establish peace in a fallen world given to chaos, disharmony, disorder, and violence? Micah 6:8 tells us:

He has showed you, O man, what is good.
And what does the Lord require of you?
To act justly and to love mercy and to walk
humbly with your God.

The prophet tells us that God has *showed* us, not simply told us, but showed us what is good. And how has God shown us justice, mercy, and humility? In the person, life, ministry, death, and resurrection of Jesus Christ. As the Prince of Peace, Christ came to destroy sin and reestablish peace and order in creation.

Orlando E. Costas observed that many English Bible translations prefer the term "righteousness" over "justice" in their translation of the Greek word *dikaiosyne*. "While righteousness can be an adequate translation... [*dikaiosyne*] is the most clearly technical term that the Old Testament uses to signify justice for the poor and oppressed, social justice...the term "righteousness" may be stylistically preferable but it is ideologically dangerous..."[19] In the Micah 6:8 text cited above, the Lord requires that we *do* justice. As Costas notes, justice is a term that carries

---

[19] Costas, Orlando E. *Christ Outside the Gate.* New York: Orbis Books, 1993. P. 39.

a socioethical significance on behalf of the poor and oppressed, which includes victims of domestic violence. This means that the church must be a voice for the voiceless, an advocate for the oppressed, and seek peace for the victimized.

The Christian Response

Violence disrupts God's design for humanity and creation. The believer is called to actively promote justice. The church must develop both short-term and long-term approaches. In the short-term, the safety of the victim and family members must be protected, and batterers must be held genuinely accountable for their violent actions. This can be accomplished first by listening and believing victims' stories, and second by appropriate referral of all family members to agencies poised to provide immediate aid and long-term treatment. But it is equally important for clergy to develop a long-range plan for ministering to the broken by becoming educated about abuse, wrestling with God and scripture, adopting policies that bring God's peace through justice, and training leaders and congregations in implementing an appropriate response. We must be a voice speaking into this issue – condemning all forms of advertisement, language, music, etc., that promote violence; preaching sermons, writing articles, and praying for victims of violence; educating our congregations and taking a clear stand against violence.

The church and clergy must look for deeper theological themes and truth to confront domestic violence with authority and love. We ministers must do our homework and not be satisfied with easy answers. We must grapple with the issues. We must seek wisdom and learn, teach and preach against domestic violence from the pulpit with knowledge, understanding, and grace. Domestic violence is not only a physical or social crisis. It is a crisis of the human spirit and soul. It is a fallacy to think that God wants anyone to "just cope" with it.

A Pastor's Response

Pastor Keith Galbraith is the director of a Christian ministry that provides confidential safe house shelter for high-risk victims of domestic violence. He and his family have worked tirelessly, gaining wide respect from the community in which they serve. The Rev. Galbraith is outspoken about his faith, and he is committed to victims of violence most every waking moment.

He has taken his message out of the pulpit to provide very real safety and protection to the most vulnerable and wounded. He has found that several factors are key to ensuring safety: believing and supporting the victim, maintaining confidentiality, sound theology, wise counsel, and prayer.

Beyond crisis intervention, Pastor Galbraith and his staff also ensure that basic long-term needs, such as transitional housing, vehicles, education and referrals to community support and local congregations, are met.

"How Do We Protect the Lives of Those in Danger?"
By The Rev. Keith Galbraith

I first met Mary Brown when she was brought to the shelter from a local hospital emergency room. Two of our staff had already visited her there a week after her husband had tried to kill her with a hammer. Mary had separated from her husband after years of escalating violent abuse, had gotten a job and relocated to a new apartment where she thought she was hidden and safe. She was wrong.

Returning home after the late shift, she was ambushed by her husband who had been hiding outside of her apartment. He attacked her from the rear and drove the claw side of the hammer deep into her skull. He then fled, leaving Mary for dead. Miraculously, she was discovered by a neighbor who then called 911. She was transported to our local military hospital Critical Care Unit, where the hammer was surgically removed from her skull. Several days later she was transferred to a second hospital, and we were called. The perpetrator was still at large, and the hospital staff was concerned for her safety. She was in a very fragile medical state and needed ongoing care.

When two of our staff members arrived at the hospital, they were informed that Mary's prognosis was not good. She had sustained brain damage and would most likely require ongoing care for the rest of her life. To survive such an injury was a miracle in itself. Led into Mary's room, they found a severely wounded woman lying helpless in her hospital bed. Staff members later told me that they were shocked by her first sentence to them. In a very small faint voice she said, "I believe God is going to heal me."

When Mary was finally released from the hospital to our shelter she was still very weak, could only walk with the aid of a walker, and made slow progress with many setbacks and follow-up medical appointments. What impressed me, though, from the first time I met her, was her sincere love for and faith in God. She believed that God was going to bring good out of this horrible act and that He was going to provide for her, heal her and give her a life worth living. She had a very difficult time communicating, thinking and processing information. It was a slow recuperation.

After many months at the shelter, Mary's health improved to the point where she was able to move into a transitional housing program. Her hair had begun to grow back, she was able to walk unassisted, and her mental faculties had dramatically improved.

Over a year after Mary left our shelter, I was speaking at a local social service agency. A woman approached me, stuck out her hand and, smiling, said, "Remember me? I'm Mary Brown." I almost fell over! The change was so dramatic.

Mary asked me if she could share her story at some point during my presentation. To everyone's amazement, halfway through her story she reached into a paper bag and pulled out a claw hammer to demonstrate how she had been injured. She went on to talk about how her relationship with Christ had sustained her and given her hope and how He could sustain anyone who would simply ask for His help. Mary's husband was finally captured, tried, convicted and sentenced to a long prison term for attempted murder. Today Mary is well, safe, employed, and walking with Christ.

Mary is one of hundreds of people we have worked with over the years who have endured the most unimaginable abuse. While men are also victims of domestic violence, the vast majority of victims who seek our services are women. We have sheltered women and children who have been shot, stabbed, strangled, bludgeoned, burned, raped, held prisoner, stalked, threatened, molested, deprived of food and sleep and treated in the most extreme, inhumane ways possible. Every day of the year and around the clock we receive calls from desperate people trying everything in their power to find safety. We believe that we have been called to support and serve those who are in the most serious danger of being killed or seriously wounded.

Does God Condone Abuse?

Domestic violence affects all levels of society, rich and poor, all races and religions. As a Christian ministry, we have been alarmed by some church leaders' teaching that suggests wife beating and abuse by a husband is to be endured as a part of the marriage covenant. Sadly, there is domestic violence in some Christian homes. We hope this brief "look in the Book" will help equip you with a Biblical perspective on this issue.

Does Scripture teach the principle that men may beat or abuse their wives? What examples can we find? In searching the Scriptures, there is not one example of the physical abuse of any wife by a positive Biblical role model. Neither Adam, nor Noah, nor Abraham, nor David, nor Jeremiah, nor Peter, nor James, nor John, nor anyone else in Scripture is shown striking his wife. However, God shows His heart of compassion and love in the marital relationship and exhorts husbands about how to relate to their wives.

> *Husbands, love your wives just as Christ loved*
> *the church, and gave himself up for her.*
> Ephesians 5:25

> *In this same way, husbands ought to love their*
> *wives as their own bodies. He who loves his*
> *wife loves himself.*
> Ephesians 5:28

Two misinterpretations of Scripture are often made concerning the "wife's submission doctrine." First, the passage in Ephesians, Chapter 5:21-33, has been misconstrued as an absolutist command forced upon a wife by a husband's claim to be sovereign ruler of his wife. This completely ignores the example of Christ in the passage, "The husband is the head of the wife as Christ is the head of the church, His body, of which He is the Savior." How does Christ head the church? *As its servant!* The 13th chapter of John, verses 1-17, beautifully portrays the example

Jesus set of washing the disciples' feet, then telling them that this act of servanthood was one they were to follow.

Secondly, Ephesians 5:21 is completely ignored by those who take verses out of context to use them as a tool to control. Ephesians 5:21 requires a *mutual* submission. "Submit to one another out of reverence for Christ." "Lord of the manor" and "King of the castle" are worldly, not Biblical concepts. God created men and women to rule His creation side by side, with mutual respect and love. The Biblical model for marriage can only be truly successful when the love of God is present.

> *If I speak with the tongues of men and angels*
> *but have not love, I am only a resounding gong*
> *or a clanging cymbal. Love is patient, love is*
> *kind, it does not envy, it does not boast, it is not*
> *proud, it is not rude, it is not self-seeking, it is*
> *not easily angered, it keeps no record of wrongs,*
> *it always protects, always trusts, always hopes,*
> *always perseveres; love never fails.*
> I Corinthians 13: 1, 4-8

Resorting to violence to teach a woman to "submit" to a husband's authority is a repudiation of the love of God. Those men who believe they have a scriptural right to strike their wives have perverted the Scriptures and missed the heart of God. Just as God gives a *free choice* to each of us to submit to Him, so must a man who loves God allow, but not force, his wife to make a free choice of her will to accommodate his position of leadership in the family.

In the Old Testament, one misapplied verse of Scripture has been used for centuries as a means to silence an abused spouse who has asked for intervention from church leaders. By quoting the first three words of Malachi 2:16 ("God hates divorce"), countless thousands of women have been told, in effect, "Your concerns are not valid, we cannot intervene because 'GOD HATES DIVORCE' - end of discussion. You have no other option but to suffer and submit in silence. This is your cross to bear. Thus sayeth the Lord."

A closer examination of the text, studied in the light of all Scripture, reveals God's true message.

In Malachi 2:13-16, God is rebuking *husbands*. At that time only husbands had the right to divorce. Christ even rebuked this practice in the New Testament and said it sprung from hardness of heart. (Matthew 19:1-8) God was correcting men who had "broken faith with the wife of their youth." The Bible then records what is usually only partially quoted, verse 16—"I hate divorce..." says the Lord God of Israel. The rest of that verse is usually left out—"... and I hate a man's covering himself (his wife) with violence."

If God hates violence against wives, can a church or individual Christian who ignores domestic violence remain credible?

In Proverbs 6:17, God says he hates hands that shed innocent blood. There is much blood being spilled in homes across our land today. The story of horror that many women and children live is just beginning to be told, and the American people are now responding by offering programs, opening shelters, and stiffening penalties against those who assault family members. The church must also quickly find its voice in this matter.

The Theology of Flight

When King Saul attempted on several occasions to murder David, David fled.
(I Samuel 18-28)

When King David's son raised up an army to hunt down and kill his father, David fled.
(II Samuel 13-19)

As soon as the Messiah was born, King Herod tried to have Him killed. Joseph was told by an angel of God to flee, to take the child and his mother and escape to Egypt.
(Matthew 2:13)

As soon as Jesus announced His messiahship in the synagogue of His hometown of Nazareth, the people drove Him out of town and took Him to the brow of a hill in order to throw Him down the cliff. But Jesus (ed. miraculously) walked right through the crowd. He escaped. (Luke 4: 16-30)

Near the end of His ministry, Christ would not enter Judea because the Jews wanted to kill Him, but Christ didn't come to be murdered but to freely give His life as a sacrifice.
(John 11: 50-55)

The apostle Paul escaped a plot to murder him by being let down over the city wall in a basket. (Acts 9: 23-25)

Most people agree that self-defense is acceptable in all circumstances. Yet there are those in the church who still believe and teach that a married woman is to submit to a husband's beatings, even if her life is threatened, and only pray for him. "It is your cross to bear so that he might come to the Lord," they are told. How sad and untrue.

One prevailing notion in some churches is that divorce is the unpardonable sin, and even separation is always a sinful, family-destroying act that should never be encouraged under any circumstances. Often the blame for the abuse being suffered in the home is placed on the victim, while the abusive partner is supported in his demand that a wife who has separated must return. While Family Renewal Shelter believes in working to restore marriages when possible, we recognize the need to hold those who abuse accountable before God, the church, and the community, while at the same time offering services to the victim and abuser. This often requires an extended separation with intensive counseling and accountability to allow for real change. A family torn by domestic violence needs the practical support of those they consider their spiritual family. Pastors and Christian workers can be a great part of giving this kind of care while also referring their members to appropriate community services and counseling.

Our prayer is that followers of Christ everywhere will rediscover this truth, that God is a God of love, compassion, forgiveness, and justice who holds those who harm others accountable for their actions.

David fled, Paul fled, even Christ fled to preserve their lives. The time has come that the church must reexamine the Bible to discover God's answer to domestic violence. For too long the church has sat quietly by while scores of women and children have suffered in fear and silence. We must encourage those who are suffering abuse inside and outside the church that the Gospel message is one of love, not exploitation, violence, and death. Wanting to be safe from beatings, threats, and abuse is a well-established Biblical precedent, not a sin.

Chapter Three

What Pastors Can Do

Is not this the kind of fasting I have chosen:
to loose the chains of injustice and untie the
cords of the yoke, to set the oppressed free
and break every yoke? Is it not to share
your food with the hungry and to provide
the poor wanderer with shelter – when you
see the naked, to clothe him, and not to
turn away from your own flesh and blood?
Isaiah 58:6-7

My father served as a pastor and missionary for more than 50 years. Through this time, we had many conversations about the rights, responsibilities and authority of the clergy. The right to marry, to bury, to hold confidences, to "rightly divide" the Word of God...

There was a time in my father's life when he learned that violence was occurring in the home of a young family whom he knew intimately. His heart was torn. In no way did he support the violence. He felt compelled to protect this young woman and their small children. He was shocked and appalled at the behavior of this husband. After much thought and prayer, he came up with what he thought to be the solution: to have weekly meetings with this young man and mentor him into manhood through the kind of servant leadership that he had demonstrated in our family home.

Sadly, the abuse continued in this family's home; it only became more cleverly disguised. The husband threatened his wife with death if she ever again disclosed what he was doing to her. She became more sullen and withdrawn, and he became more cooperative and seemingly appreciative of the pastor's helpful suggestions during their time together. Yet, when he came home from these times, he would ridicule and mimic the pastor and the Christian faith. These displays by her husband served to deeply break the heart of the young woman and subject her children to further abuse. Unwittingly, the pastor was colluding with the abuser.

I asked my father why he could not recommend that she leave him and find safety. He replied, obviously anguished, "Nancy, I am in the business of making marriages, not seeing them break up."

Today, my father would respond very differently. This chapter tells a story of someone who did.

The Rev. Dr. Randy J. Bridges was ordained at Southern Hills Baptist Church in Boulder, Colorado, in 1972. He has a Ph.D. in Christian Education from Biola University, and an M.A. from Talbot Theological Seminary. Currently he is President of Puget Sound Christian College, and on the national faculty of Leadership Training for Mission America.

"One Couple's Story"
By The Rev. Dr. Randy J. Bridges

Karen and Bob sat quietly in my office, waiting for our discussion to begin – I always like to meet with newlyweds a few months into their marriages to see how things are going. I recalled that in pre-marital counseling Karen had remained fairly quiet, though always pleasant. Bob had had a hearty handshake, broad shoulders, and a ready smile. I had liked them both and thought them to be a good match.

I offered them coffee and began our time with a word of prayer. We visited for awhile and then I asked how marriage was. Instantly, Karen's face flushed and her eyes filled with tears. She withdrew into a moment of silence and then smiled and proclaimed, "It is really good!" She affirmed her husband Bob, and quickly launched into a list of his greatest attributes, stroking his arm affectionately.

Not willing to overlook the tears, I inquired about them. Hastily, Bob interrupted to announce that Karen was pregnant and more emotional than ever. I offered my congratulations and invited them over for dinner the following week. I was confused. Her tears did not seem to be tears of joy, nor did I know her to be exceptionally emotional. She had barely spoken a word.

During the week, Karen called me privately to talk about Bob's anger and frustration. She was sure it was her fault and wanted to know how to be a "better" Christian wife. I assured her that it was probably just the jitters of having a baby on the way and the responsibility of the future. We agreed that I would call Bob and set a time for dinner so I could evaluate his situation for myself.

We had arranged dinner together for Saturday night, but Karen called at the last minute to say she wasn't feeling well and that they would like to reschedule. The conversation continued on about the moodiness and sullen attitude that Bob sometimes displayed. I looked for her at church the next morning, but neither of them was there.

Time passed quickly as I became involved in more ministry in the church. Karen and Bob seemed to be busy with work and family. When we did talk after Sunday services, it was mostly Bob describing how his new business ventures were developing. In a few months, the baby came. Bob and Karen looked happy, and I felt that they had passed the difficult spot in their relationship and were on their way to a full life together. I suggested that we try another run at having dinner together, and we scheduled a Saturday evening a few weeks out.

One afternoon, Karen called and frantically shared that Bob had mistreated their baby. Her story seemed so out of character for Bob. I calmed her down, assured her that Bob was probably just under a great deal of pressure, and reminded her that the emotional adjustment to the role of mother takes time. She agreed that it was a huge adjustment and seemed to be satisfied that the future was brighter than she had painted it.

As always happens for pastors, the phone rang in the early hours of the morning. It was Bob stating that he and Karen had had a misunderstanding. She wanted to call the police, but he had begged her for a chance to call me, "his pastor," first. He wanted to know if they could see me right away.

When they arrived at the office, Bob said he hadn't intended to hurt her, it was just that he was so afraid of losing her and had meant to show her how much he loved her. "It just happened," was his comment. Her eyes were red. Her lips were beginning to swell, and bruise marks had already appeared on her arms where he had gripped her with both of his hands so tightly that the fingerprints remained. I was furious!

Nevertheless, I thought our time together went well. The anger and fear seemed to dissipate as we went along. Bob was very passive and seemed repentant and in deep grief. He made promises that seemed open and honest. We worked out a plan for them to connect with church friends and begin the process of getting them some help.

They agreed to this plan, and assured me that they were going to be just fine and that a good sleep would change everything. Bob came to Karen's side and embraced her and stroked her hair. He apologized for getting me in the middle of all of this, thanked me, and then stood up to leave. Karen's face fell, but she insisted once again she would be fine, joined in making the apology, and said she would call in the morning.

As they drove away, my mind was racing. What should I do? Call the police? Should I have made Bob leave the home? What about the next day? Was this marriage going to make it? Was it one of the ones you hear about in the news where someone would lose their life? Had we done enough? Why had Karen looked so fearful upon leaving? Should we call her parents? Was this the first time something like this had happened? What about the baby? Had I missed something in pre-marital counseling? I felt helpless and afraid.

The agonizing questions lasted the entire next day. My prayers were fervent for wisdom, direction, peace and safety for all of us. I decided to call a professional counselor who was a member in our church. I knew I needed guidance. He insisted I call two numbers immediately, to help me learn more about what to expect in situations of abuse, and also so that I would have appropriate referral numbers to give to Karen and Bob. One number was for an advocate for victims of domestic violence, and the other was for a counselor who provides treatment and counseling for men who are violent.

I had really hoped that, for starters, he would see them together. When I mentioned that, I was taken aback with his reply. "Couples counseling is not an appropriate course of action when there has been violence in the marriage. I know that marriage, and this couple in particular, is very important to you, but where violence and abuse has occurred in a marriage or dating relationship, the focus must first be on safety for the ones who are being hurt. Very often, couples counseling, or even the process of individual counseling, can actually serve to escalate the violence and endanger a woman's life further." I assured the counselor that I was going to keep a very close eye on this couple and was pretty sure that he wouldn't dare hit her ever again. What a ridiculous statement I had just made, and somewhere in my heart I knew it was untrue. But I wanted to believe that a "good Christian man" would not be capable of further harm.

The counselor was gracious, but encouraged me to do some reading and to learn about domestic violence. He told us that clearly Bob was using his fists first and then his kindness to control Karen and that unless she found an absolutely safe place to disclose what had happened to her and to share how she was feeling, she would not be safe physically, emotionally, or spiritually in that marriage. An advocate would help her develop a safety plan, provide a confidential ear, and listen to her carefully to help her figure out what would be best for her to do next.

A counselor who provides treatment for abusive men would work to increase Karen's safety as well, but in a different way. He would provide Bob with counseling in a group with other offenders, to hold Bob accountable for his violence and encourage him to take responsibility for changing his behavior. Bob had broken his vows to his wife to "love, honor and cherish 'til death do us part." If there were to be restoration of their marriage, Bob would first have to be reconciled to God and be accountable for his behavior. He would have to demonstrate change in order for Karen to ever be able to trust or respect him again.

The counselor said that couples counseling would only be appropriate after Karen's safety was assured and Bob had undergone treatment – maybe a year or a year-and-a-half from now. He encouraged me to stay in relationship with them. He emphasized that God does not condone abuse – ever, that Karen is precious to her Maker, and that Bob must genuinely repent of his sin in order to be reconciled to God. We could play an important part in the restoration of this marriage, he told us, but first steps must be taken first. Karen's safety and Bob's treatment must be given priority. The other option would be to report this incident to the police. Violence against a spouse or an intimate partner is a crime. Bob would be arrested and sent to jail or court-ordered into treatment.

Ultimately Karen made her own choice. She filed for a restraining order and moved out to a confidential location known only to me. We were on our way to court-mandated domestic violence programs, a long separation, and much personal pain on both sides before reconciliation would take place.

After the legal and civil actions began to unfold, I started to understand the gravity of the situation. I resolved to take the advice of the counselor and realized that it was critical that we as a church understand this whole process from a Biblical perspective. 2 Timothy 4:2 reads, "Preach the Word: be prepared in season and out of season; correct, rebuke and encourage~ with great patience and careful instruction." We were familiar with the theology of suffering and forgiveness, but is that what God intended for Karen within the confines of her marriage to Bob? We knew that we needed more education about domestic violence and we needed to search the Scriptures for clear direction from the Lord.

After much study, prayer, and discussion, I recommended several resolutions to stop abuse in the church. In general, they are contained in these statements:[20]

> The Bible specifically condemns murder, enslavement, rape, incest, physical assault, mutilation, verbal and emotional abuse, threats and intimidation. God's Word provides absolutely no warrant for the violation or oppression of women. Neither should culture or tradition be allowed to contradict scripture.
>
> The church is called:
> To *denounce these evils* in its ministry of public proclamation;
> To *protect and provide* for those in need of safety;
> To *offer healing* for those wounded in body, mind and soul;
> To *admonish offenders*, in cooperation with civil authorities, guiding and restoring them until new patterns of behavior are verified.

Then I set about to establish several general practices to assure clear leadership in these difficult situations.

Safety First

As a pastor faced with a specific family, a specific marriage in trouble, I was called to practical action. I was still uncertain what to do. The news is always reporting stories of domestic violence that end in someone's death. I was afraid for Karen. Would Bob take her life~ or his? Would my life or my family's life be threatened as a result of "interfering?"

We had said that we would protect and provide for those in need of safety. It was time to learn exactly what that meant. Somehow I knew that in order to help Karen, I would not be able to let Bob know about it. He clearly felt threatened when he thought she was talking to someone about her home life, and we must be very careful not to jeopardize her safety.

---

[20]Quote from a resolution passed unanimously by the 11th General Assembly of World Evangelical Alliance (WEA)—May 2001.

I realized how many beliefs exist entitling a husband to "rule" his house in any way he would want.

"A man's home is his castle."

"God wants me to be the Head of the home."

"I'll show her who is boss."

This was not going to be as easy as I had hoped, yet the work of the gospel is to be on the side of the brokenhearted.

The Lord is close to the brokenhearted and saves those who are crushed in spirit.
Psalm 34:18

He heals the brokenhearted and binds up their wounds.
Psalm 147:3

I felt the challenge to:

• Hear more of Karen's story, to really listen to her and to stand with her, believing her. I knew it would be hard for me to stand by and take the lead from Karen, but I was coming to realize that she knows much more about keeping safe than I ever could.

• Make Karen's safety a priority. Physically she needed to be assured that she would not be hurt again. Emotionally she needed to be supported and reassured that she did not deserve to be treated in this way~ ever. Spiritually she would need to hear that this was not God's will for her life and that God was not on the side of those who abuse others. God loved her and would not abandon her.

• Involve others in this process. I was struck with the complexity of this issue and felt overwhelming gratitude for shelters and for the counselors who work there. I hoped I would be able to find a domestic violence treatment provider who would be able to hold Bob accountable to stop his violent behavior. I could see that it could take a long time to change his mindset. What a tough job they had!

• Become educated about the resources in my community and be prepared for such incidents in the future.

• Commit myself to prayer for all the other "Karen-and-Bobs" in our congregations.

Accountability

*Nothing in all creation is hidden from God's sight.
Everything is uncovered and laid bare before the
eyes of him to whom we must give account.*
Hebrews 4:13

*Seek the Lord while he may be found; call on him
while he is near. Let the wicked forsake his way
and the evil man his thoughts. Let him turn to the
Lord and he will have mercy on him, and to our
God, for he will freely pardon.*
Isaiah 55: 6-7

*Whoever loves discipline loves knowledge, but he
who hates correction is stupid.*
Proverbs 12:1

If Karen had been struck by a stranger, we would not have hesitated to call the police. We would never have stopped to think whether she had "provoked" the attack. We would have taken immediate action to bring her attacker to justice under the law. Why, then, is it any different when the attack comes from her husband? Why is not even more serious? Why do we feel we need to cover it up so quickly?

Just as a stranger would be held accountable for his actions, so must her husband be. If he refuses to voluntarily enter a treatment program, he must be court-ordered to do so. Pastoral counseling does not substitute for a formal treatment/accountability program. There are many complicating factors in the pastoral relationship that preclude effective accountability: lack of therapeutic training; the difficulty a non-therapist has in unmasking the

"If an enemy were insulting me, I could endure it; if a foe were raising himself against me, I could hide from him. But it is you, a man like myself, a companion, my close friend, with whom I once enjoyed sweet fellowship as we walked with the throng at the house of God."

Psalm 55: 12-14

"good guy face" so often adopted by the abuser; the broad scope of the pastor/parishioner relationship that makes it difficult to focus solely on accountability; the fact that both husband and wife may be continuing in relationship with the pastor and the church; and the need to focus on safety first.

I could just imagine that Bob would now begin to volunteer at our feeding program, or increase his tithe. He might begin to attend our men's ministry events. Certainly, all of these things are desirable, but not to take the place of the expectation that he stop abusing his wife. I could envision Bob trying to solicit our sympathy by getting more involved at the church, possibly trying to shortcut the work of changing his behavior, or trying to encourage me to break confidentiality about Karen's whereabouts. But I had seen Karen myself. She had been scared and badly wounded and I was determined never to let that happen to her again, if I had anything to say about it. I cared about Bob and was committed to him and to his faith; his behavior was intolerable and must change. In order for him to grow to be strong in the Lord, he would need to see himself clearly and learn the Christian disciplines of kindness, respect, love and the sacrifice of leadership. He would find accountability in a formal treatment program and in our consistent love and regard for him while he underwent treatment.

Reconciliation

"None of these changes or confrontations were easy. They didn't just happen. They came by the vehicle of pain, sweat and tears. They came about through the conscious resolution that [he] made to take responsibility for himself, to make peace with his parents, to save his marriage and to keep his family. They came at a high price, the sacrifice of himself. He had to lose his life in order to find it."[21]

I learned some hard lessons about reconciliation:
Reconciliation is NOT the acceptance of a quick apology.
It is NOT returning to the way things were~ keeping the status quo.
It is NOT premature forgiveness and the blind hope that everything will be different next time.

---

[21] Sitzer, M'Liss & Katherine Hale. *Called to Account*. Seattle, WA: Seal Press, 1987, p.129.

Reconciliation requires first a confession of sin. "Therefore confess your sins to each other and pray for each other, so that you may be healed." (James 5:16) Nothing is hidden from God, yet we often try to hide the truth from ourselves. Confession involves admitting the exact nature of our wrong. Confession opens the door to repentance; true repentance brings God's forgiveness.

Healing is not instantaneous, but repentance and forgiveness begin to move us from a place of pain and bondage to a place of joy and freedom. Moving from power and control to equality, respect and the power of love is essential for reconciliation of relationship (See Appendix B, page 74-75, for diagrams illustrating this.) Where equality is lacking, abuse will flourish.

Reconciliation is possible between man and God because God is love. Reconciliation is possible between man and woman with God's love, made manifest in a mutually respectful and loving relationship.

The bottom line is that our lives as Christians must reflect the love of Christ. Paul quite clearly describes how we are to live in relationship with others. 1 Corinthians 13: 4-8 tells us of the attributes of a healthy, loving relationship:

Love is patient

Love is kind

It does not envy

It does not boast

It is not proud

It is not rude

It is not self-seeking

It is not easily angered

It keeps no record of wrongs.

Love does not delight in evil but rejoices with the truth.

It always protects, always trusts, always hopes, always perseveres,

Love never fails.

There is no room for violence in this definition of love.

Conclusion

What the Lord Requires of Us

He has showed you, O man, what is good.
And what does the LORD require of you?
To act justly and to love mercy and
to walk humbly with your God.
Micah 6:8

Violence in a marriage breaks the vows to love, honor and cherish. It creates fear and chaos. It destroys hope and mocks trust. Domestic violence impacts all of us.

It is imperative to understand that no one deserves to be beaten or abused. Choosing to marry is not choosing to be abused or controlled. And choosing the safety of distance is not the same as abandoning the marriage vows. If there is violence in a relationship, the problem lies with the abuser. It is not a problem in the relationship. Violence is a learned behavior and therefore it can be unlearned. Therein lies the hope. An individual who is abusing must make changes. With those changes comes an opportunity to experience relationship based on honor and respect.

Dr. Catherine Clark Kroeger says:

> "Quite correctly, evangelicals maintain a high view of the Christian home and seek to build strong families. This is commendable, but it is important that a biblical perspective be offered. In the Bible, one of the features most strongly emphasized for godly homes is that of safety. Believers are promised that they may dwell in safety, lie down to sleep in safety and that their homes will be free of terror and violence.

'My people will abide in a peaceful habitation,
in secure dwellings, and in quiet resting places.'
(Isaiah 32:18)

The theme is a recurrent one. Indeed, the
prophet Isaiah maintains that peace in the home,
safety and righteousness are the inheritance of
the believer (Isaiah 54:13-17). Faithful teaching
on the Christian family must include at least as
much proclamation of these aspects as is accord-
ed in Scripture."[22]

The Bible clearly indicates that God wants marriage to last a lifetime in peace, safety and righteousness. The Church is called to uphold these principles through the provision of safety, accountability, and avenues for mourning and reconciliation. May our homes, our sanctuaries and our communities be safer places as a result of our responses to domestic violence.

[22] Dr. Catherine Clark Kroeger, personal correspondence with author, August, 2003.

Appendix A

Congregational Responses

Again I looked and saw all the oppression
that was taking place under the sun: I saw
the tears of the oppressed~ and they have no
comforter; power was on the side of their
oppressors~ and they have no comforter.
Ecclesiastes 4:1

I believe that we have a growing body of Christian believers who are rising up with a strong voice that says, "No more!" They are the comforters. They are the ones that are coming alongside the broken and bruised with the words of comfort that say:

"I am so sorry this has happened to you."
"You deserve to be treated with dignity and respect."
"You are precious to God. You are precious to me."

They are opening their hearts and their pockets to provide resources for the countless women and children left homeless, destitute, relocated and afraid.

Those who are being violent and abusive are being challenged rather than applauded. It is understood that those who witness abuse in their childhood are more likely to become our next abusers.[23] Clearly, domestic violence is a learned behavior and must be unlearned. Many abusers have endured horrific experiences of abuse themselves or witnessed their mothers being abused. The trauma remains and must be reduced in order for healing to take place. They must experience the faithfulness of God and the consistency of the Body of Christ in saying "no" to abuse, but "yes" to the one who has abused. Abusers need to know that they will be held accountable for their abuse and that God, through the congregation, will walk with them on their journey. The love of God transforms hearts and enables us all to move from the love of power to the power of love.

Stories have been included in this chapter that illustrate various congregational responses to domestic violence. The work of Christ is being carried out all over the world; it is being manifested in our congregations.

[23] Jaffe et al. 1986: cf. Statistics Canada 1993

A Christian Woman's Plea

Karla S. McElroy serves as the assistant to the provost for Puget Sound Christian College and as an instructor for women's issues in ministry. She implores congregations to keep their eyes, ears, and hearts open to signs of abuse, and to be prepared to respond with love.

"We Must Do What We Can"
By Karla S. McElroy

It was simply another piece of unsolicited advertising – junk mail. Yet the words caught my attention and as a result, I will never be the same.

As the administrative assistant to the academic dean of a small Christian college, my job includes scheduling speakers for weekly chapels. For the most part I call people suggested by others, but when I read the brochure that described the ministry of Northwest Family Life Learning and Counseling Center (NWFL), I was compelled to contact the director to see if she would be interested in speaking to our students and staff. Not only did she come, share her life story and talk one-on-one with several students and faculty, but since then Nancy Murphy has spoken annually, taught part-time and welcomed students as interns at NWFL.

I am the mother of a 23-year-old daughter. For more than thirty years I have served with women, taught women in formal and informal settings, and have been in ministry both stateside and overseas. I have been committed to the health of Christian women my entire life, yet to be recently introduced to the crime of domestic violence has refocused my heart. Learning that many women in this world are caring for their families and serving the kingdom while enduring great pain has overwhelmed me. My own home has always been a haven. I have had what I call a "white picket fence" life. It breaks my heart to realize how many women and children are emotionally and physically abused on a regular basis by the very ones who should nurture and protect them.

I am sickened to think that the numbers are as great within the church as outside of it. Often the sin of abuse is compounded by church leaders who won't address the problem because they refuse to be a part of the desperately needed healing, or they don't recognize the signs. The numbers are staggering: One in four women is a victim of abuse. I can no longer sit in a room of twenty women without being painfully aware that at least four or five of them are afraid of their boyfriends or husbands. To ignore the problem is to be a part of the problem, and to allow abuse is to be an abuser.

The Lord is making my heart sensitive to all that I am learning and I cannot ignore His calling. I can help spread the word by telling everyone in my corner of the world how serious the problem of domestic violence is. I can help by lending my time and energies toward helping in whatever ways the Lord opens to me. I can help by being a constant reminder that the victims of domestic violence are God's suffering children whose voices must be heard.

So many people have opened their ears and hearts to those who suffer violence in their homes. Some refuse. Some simply haven't heard. But you have – just by opening this book, by reading it. I thank you for that, and I pray that you will act as the Lord is leading you to help bind up the broken-hearted, to be His hands that will help set the captives free, to share His hope and healing.

Are you a pastor? A church leader? Women's director? Youth leader? Do you know the Lord and desire to be a minister of His grace? Then please, watch for the signs of unhealthy relationships, encourage women to take action that will first ensure safety, be willing to intervene with the goal of redeemed and restored relationships, teach and model godly relationships for young women and men. We must all do what we can.

A Congregation Reaches Out

Cindy S. Bohnett is active in her church doing counseling and teaching. She is on the Board of Directors for a Christian agency that works with families touched by domestic violence and enjoys community work and ministry with her husband through the Bohnett Memorial Foundation. Her story illustrates how a congregation can impact generations by rescuing those suffering in homes of abuse. The church members who reached out to 14-year old Cindy and her siblings offer a powerful example of true Christian families. Their support helped inspire her healing journey.

"One Family's Journey"
By Cindy S. Bohnett

I was raised in an abusive home. At the time I would have simply called it "strict" or have said my father drank too much. For as far back as I can remember every detail of my life was controlled and full of unreasonable rules that had a way of changing, for no apparent reason, depending on "dad's mood." Everyone in my home walked on eggshells as we lived in fear of dad flying into a rage and hurting someone.

When I was fourteen, a friend invited me to go to church with her family, and it was there that I began a spiritual journey of healing the wounds of abuse. I remember coming home from church one Sunday and telling my parents that I had become a Christian, naively thinking that they would be happy or at least supportive. My father instead flew into a rage and told me he would rather have me tell him I was on drugs or pregnant! I understand now that he was simply afraid that I was going to get into something that he could not control. He was right in a way. I took my newfound faith very seriously, reading my Bible, going to church every time I could and witnessing to my friends. The more he persecuted me, the closer I clung to God, who was becoming to me the Father I had always desired.

During my teen years I started taking my younger brother and sister with me to church and soon they also decided to become followers of Christ. I am not sure if the people in our church body knew the extent of what was going on in our home but I am so thankful for God's provision of surrogate Christian families. They came along side of us, drove us to church, included us in their families and of course prayed for and with us. Through them, we were able to see a different model o family and most of all to gain a sense of hope that God could break the generational patterns of addiction and abuse.

After my siblings and I were married, we got together with our spouses and prayed that God would break this generational sin in our family. Our desire was that it would stop with us and we would not pass this "curse" on to our children and our children's children. Between us, we have 10 kids and we have been very motivated to work on our relationships with one another even though it had never been taught to us how exactly to do that. We also started new family traditions so that all of us would get together twice a year. We wanted our children to see genuine Christian relationship modeled through their extended family.

After we three children left home, my mother also started attending church and became a Christian. She was counseled by well-meaning Christian leaders to stay with my dad and "influence him through her godly life." Hopefully he would see the light and change his evil ways. After 43 years of an abusive marriage, she was only "allowed" to go to the grocery store on Thursdays between 9 and 10. She was my father's prisoner in her own home. We felt very helpless; we had no way to contact her that was safe for her or for us. All we could do was pray that God would bring the truth to light and would provide a way of escape for my mother.

The final straw came when my father began medicating her with his prescription drugs to "calm her down." She would lie on the floor for days unable to eat. I will never forget the day she called from the grocery store and asked me to help her. I had waited a long time for that phone call! Within three weeks we had developed a safety plan and came up with a way to rescue her. After a year in hiding, I am thankful to say that she has started a new life of freedom and family. Her faith continues to be strong and her love for her children and grandchildren has finally had an opportunity to grow and be realized.

I sought out any and all resources that would be of help to our family during this difficult time and was disappointed with the lack of helpful material in the Christian community on this issue. Domestic violence is a topic that is close to the heart of God, and I know it grieves Him to see the pain it continues to bring to His children. We in the church have a responsibility to educate our body about domestic violence. It is in every pew, in every church, in every town.

I know firsthand that if someone you care about is in the situation of domestic violence, it can be difficult to know how to help. Often the most important thing you can do is listen. You may be privileged to be the one to carry some of the story and lighten their burden. Don't be afraid to sometimes ask the tough questions to help bring the suffering out of the closet and let the truth be known. A person experiencing abuse suffers in isolation. Don't withdraw; if you have made the effort to maintain contact, you may be the only person they can call. Be prepared to help. Be aware of the various resources in your community and be educated on the issue of domestic violence. Be willing to stand with them in finding an advocate to help them to safety. And of course, pray for God's intervention and light. He will provide the wisdom and strength to navigate the difficult path towards healing, strength, faith, and wholeness.

A Pastor's Wife's Story

Mrs. Gail J. Mullen is a graduate of Northwest College with a business degree in Organizational Communication. She works in ministry alongside her husband planning and implementing programs within the ministry. Her first ministry has always been her family. She is consistent in managing every area of her life as an example of Christ. Mrs. Mullen's story demonstrates that, when Christ is brought into the family for the first time, hope enters in.

"Is There Any Hope?"
By Mrs. Gail J. Mullen

I grew up in a time when there was a great stigma against families who voiced domestic violence to the community. You were embarrassed and ashamed if you and your household were experiencing varying types of abuse within the home. Far too many families put on the "happy face," whether it was swollen or not, and life went on as usual. Often "business as usual" meant abuse, under various names – sexual, physical, mental, or emotional abuse. As I have often said, "Hurting people hurt people."

My stepfather walked in the abusive footsteps of his own father. His mother had had a nervous breakdown from the physical abuse in the home and had to be hospitalized. My dad was pulled out of school in the fourth grade in order to help with his sister and brother at home, while his father lived the life of a ladies' man.

As a child, I can vividly remember the violence inflicted upon my mother by my father. My father's way to justify his abusive actions was to think that he was bringing order to the family, to get them in shape. But in shape for what?! My mother was a homebody who just wanted to be a wife and mom. Dad would beat us children so badly that marks from the strap covered the backs of our entire bodies. No one really used the words "child abuse" when I was growing up. If my mother objected, my dad would verbally and physically abuse her too. He would tell her that these children are going to be raised right even if he had to whip them every day. My dad couldn't understand why my mother was always calling the police and why my siblings would run in fear from him.

I vividly remember one of the many incidents of abuse I witnessed as a child. It was on a summer Minnesota evening. My dad had my brother and me in the car to pick up my mom at the hospital. She had just given birth to a third child. I was so excited that I had a new baby sister! My mom had to pick up a prescription on the way home, so my dad stopped at a drugstore not far from where we lived. The traffic was heavy, so he told my mom to go get her prescription while we waited in the car. I remember holding my new little sister thinking how soft her little hands felt as she lay in my arms sleeping.

Everything was quiet in the car while my mother was in the store. We knew not to make noise or it would set my dad off in a rage. It seemed like we waited for only a short period of time, but my dad began to cuss about the length of time my mom was in the store. As soon as my mother left the store heading toward the car, he asked her what took her so long? I could see fear written all over my mother's face, as my dad approached her in broad daylight and beat her outside of the car, in the heavy traffic hour. My brother and I cried and pleaded with him not to beat our mom, but our cries fell on deaf ears. People stopped their cars and screamed at my dad that they were going to call the police.

He threw our crying mom in the car and sped away to our house. What a horrible homecoming not only for my mom, but also for my new baby sister as well! What should have been a joyous occasion was marred with a horrible act of physical violence. Each of us children developed our own coping mechanisms to deal with the violence in our home. At an early age I went underground, emotionally. I used to stand in front of the mirror in my bedroom and act like I was on stage. I would do scenes of a life far removed from the pain and ugliness I was actually experiencing. As I approached my pre-teen years, my coping mechanism was to be dad's little girl who always did the right things to keep out of trouble. I had over time developed a false sense of devotion to my father. For his birthday parties, I would encourage my sisters and brother to make these memorable occasions for daddy.

I don't remember the precise time in my childhood that my mother accepted Jesus Christ as her personal Savior. After that, she would take us to church, despite my father's disapproval of religion. At times we would hear him from our bedroom cussing at her about trying to be religious. (He was a Baptist, but to him praying and speaking in tongues was radical.)

As an adult I can remember the happiest day of my childhood was not Christmas or the huge family Thanksgiving meals, but it was the day my mother found the strength to say mentally, emotionally, and physically, "Enough is enough is enough!" That was the major turning point in my childhood.

Eventually I also accepted Christ as my personal Savior and married a wonderful man who not only had an unfailing love for Christ, but he loved me in spite of my many hang-ups. I remember that when my husband first asked me to marry him, I said no. I thought since there were no successful long-term marriages in my family, ours would probably last about five years. Thankfully he convinced me, and we have been married for 36 years; we have three living children, and two children that are with the Lord.

My husband and I moved to Seattle, Washington with our sons. One day my mother called and asked me to come home because my dad was diagnosed with cancer and had only a matter of days or weeks to live. Emotions I had not realized as an adult began to surface - coldness, indifference. I felt no remorse that I had no feelings for my father. One day, after my husband had prayed and ministered to me, I began to feel the loving arms of my heavenly Father embrace me. Up to this point, I had not wanted to ask God to forgive me for my bitterness against my dying father. But our Father God is so wonderful in His approach to His children. One night I couldn't sleep, so I got up while the house was quiet and peaceful. I sat by an open window and tears began to stream down my face and I prayed, "Father, I don't know how to forgive this man I call dad. The pain is too deep, and the memories are too vivid. I thought I really loved him, but now my emotions are hollow and empty. Please give me the strength to want to care about him dying!"

A few days later, I began to prepare to go to Minneapolis to be with the rest of my family. I thought that when I got to the hospital I would settle the matter, once and for all, telling him about the pain he had inflicted upon me as a child. But by the time I got to the hospital, unbeknownst to me, my father had accepted Jesus Christ as his personal Savior. I was shocked beyond words. Not only had he accepted Christ, but he also had acknowledged to every family member the wrong that he had inflicted and asked for forgiveness. I was so stunned that words totally escaped me. I returned home to Seattle, never telling my father what I had planned to tell him. Instead, I carried home with me a sense of true, genuine reconciliation. A few days after coming home, my father went home to be with the Lord. His acceptance of Christ as his personal Savior was God's grace to me.

There comes a time when we must realize that to be free of the results of violence and abuse in our lives, of feeling that we have no value, of jeopardizing our own lives and the lives of our children, we must gather the courage to seek help outside of ourselves. Change takes courage and time. Often, when we have been violated and abused, it is impossible for us to comprehend that even those who have inflicted pain, misery, emotional and physical anguish, and sometimes death to those we love, can change. Lasting change can only take place with the sovereign help and intervention of our heavenly Father.

A Church Elder Speaks

Judge David A. Steiner is married, has two children and serves as an elder at Crossroads Bible Church in Bellevue, Washington. He was appointed to the King County District Court bench in 1996. In 2000, he pushed for and assisted in the creation of a specialized domestic violence court. He currently serves as one of two judges in that court. Judge Steiner's story shows that the apparently conflicting values of intolerance of domestic violence and redemption of the abuser can be held equally side-by-side.

"Justice and Reconciliation"
By Judge David A. Steiner

As a Judge dealing with domestic violence cases, I am presented with two different concerns. One primary role of the court is to see that justice is served. The second primary concern in a criminal domestic violence case is always victim safety. Unfortunately, in the courts, victim safety is often viewed as a "competing interest" to family reconciliation.

As a church elder I also must deal with domestic violence victims' fears about returning to home and marriage following a history of abuse. One of the weaknesses in many churches is the failure to uncover the domestic violence until the victim has already reached a point where she feels compelled to leave. Thus, pastors and elders often see these cases only when the partners have already started using the word "divorce," at the point when reconciliation seems only a distant possibility.

Though there is a perception of a conflict between the approach of the church and that of the courts, closer examination reveals a commonality of underlying goals. Both the church and the courts should pursue and encourage strong family relationships. Both the church and the courts should pursue and encourage safety and dignity for each family member. To accomplish these goals, both the church and the courts must become intolerant of domestic violence. This is impossible for the church as long as we maintain a position that says marriages must be maintained at all costs.

Yet, intolerance to domestic violence is not enough. Both the church and the courts must continue to work for the redemption of men and women. While this role is obvious for the churches, the goal of strong families will not be met if our courts are too ready to permanently split families with a history of domestic violence.

As an elder and as a Judge, I believe strongly in the need for the intervention of the church and the courts when domestic violence is discovered. When domestic violence is confronted with intolerance, and work is undertaken to promote the redemption of the batterer, there is reason to hope.

Appendix B

Resources

How to Recognize a Victim of Domestic Violence [24]

Domestic violence and abuse cuts across all social, economic, racial, religious, and age barriers. The traditional concept of the "battered wife" doesn't take into account the many other abuse victims in our community. As you are in relationship with families in your church community, there are several abuse warning signs of which you can be aware. The following list can be helpful in identifying possible abuse:

- Does she seem to have unexplained injuries?
- Does she seem to be "sick" often?
- Does she live in fear of her partner?
- Is she afraid to be late getting home?
- Does her description of her intimate relationship just not ring true?
- Does she feel that she doesn't deserve to be treated any better?
- Does she excuse the abuse by saying it is probably her fault?
- Does she express fear of her partner's anger?
- Does she accept the responsibility for his actions?
- Does she believe she should hold the relationship together, no matter what he does?
- Does she seem to be consumed with keeping her partner from getting angry?
- Does she worry that someone might find out about the problems in the relationship?
- Does she describe all the problems in the relationship as being her fault?
- Does she seem cut off from friends, family, social life, education, work or church?
- Does she keep hoping that the relationship will improve and he will see how he needs to change?
- Does she suffer from feelings of guilt, depression, anger and failure because of her partner's actions?
- Does she find herself the victim of his extreme jealousies, always trying to justify her every move?
- Are her movements constantly tracked by her partner?
- Do her children seem to either cling to her as if trying to protect her, or order her around and treat her disrespectfully?

[24] Based on handout from Family Renewal Shelter, Tacoma, Washington. 253-475-9010, www.domesticviolencehelp.org Used with permission.

What Can I Do to Help Her?

Keep in mind the goals:

- *Safety* for the woman and the children;
- *Accountability* for the abuser;
- *Restoration* of individuals, and if possible, relationships or if not possible, *mourning* the loss of the relationships.[25]

Here are some suggestions that pastors have found helpful in working with battered women:

- Be alert, but not suspicious; long sleeves in summer, sunglasses indoors, withdrawal from social occasions as well as unexplained injuries can be signs of battering.

- Demonstrate genuine concern; the victim needs to know you care about her as an individual, that you are her friend.

- Listen and believe; be ready to hear whatever she has to say, for as long as it takes her to say it.

- Be patient; don't expect her to move quickly through the process of changing.

- Be trustworthy and calm; the victim needs to know she can open up to you.

- Encourage her to think about a safety plan. This might include her setting aside some money, copies of important papers for her and her children, a change of clothes hidden or in care of a friend. It could also include a plan about how to exit the house the next time the abuser is violent, as well as considerations of what to do about the children if they are at school, if they are asleep, etc. Safety planning is an ongoing process that offers practical assistance and also helps her stay in touch with the reality of the abuser's violence.

- Educate yourself; know the available services in your area and the procedure to follow in calling for law enforcement or agency help.

- Know where the shelters are. A good phone number for this information is 1-800-799-7233 (or 1-800-787-3224 TDD).

[25] Based on "Responding to Domestic Violence: Guidelines for Pastors – working with battered women." FaithTrust Institute, Seattle, WA, www.faithtrustinstitute.org

- Reassure the children.

- Help the victim find a safe place, with you, or elsewhere. Decide how you will deal with the abuser if he comes around.

- Encourage the victim, but realize that she must make her own choices.

- Let her know that what the abuser has done to her is wrong, and that God does not want her to remain in a situation where her life and the lives of her children are in danger.

- Assure her of God's love and presence, and your commitment to walk with her.

- Protect her confidentiality, keeping your conversations with her completely private. Even well-intentioned conversations with elders or others in the church could be dangerous to her, if someone inadvertently passes information on to the abuser.

- Be a true friend; be supportive in whatever the victim does or does not do.

As in any relationship, there are things that help to build a relationship and other actions that tear it down. Here are some suggestions of what to avoid, as they are not helpful in dealing with the situation, and may in fact increase the risk of violence.

- Do not lose patience.

- Avoid judgments.

- Do not add her name to a prayer chain for any reason.

- Refrain from giving advice, telling her that you would never put up with such treatment, or that she is wrong for staying in the situation.

- Do not try to talk to her partner or approach him on your own.

- Do not try to intervene in the middle of a violent episode.

What Can I Do to Help Him? [26]

It is very important that you not initiate a conversation about domestic violence with the abuser. If his wife has spoken with you in confidence and you bring it up with him, you are endangering her safety and the safety of the children.

If *he* approaches *you* and discloses that he has been violent and asks for your help:

Keep the goals in mind:
- *Safety* for the woman and children;
- *Accountability* for the abuser;
- *Restoration* of individuals and, if possible, relationships or *mourning* the loss of relationships.

- Express your concern. Let him know that you will support him to be accountable and to deal with his violence.

- Refer him to a treatment program designed specifically for abusers.

- Pray with him. Ask God to help him stop his violence, repent and find a new way.

- Find ways to collaborate with community agencies and law enforcement to hold him accountable.

- Address any religious questions he may have, and let him know that there is nothing in Scriptures to justify abusive behavior.

- In all dealings with him, be very careful to protect the safety of the victim. This means it is critical that you not be the one to initiate a discussion of his violence with him, and that you not give him any information about his partner if she has left the home.

[26] Adapted from "Responding to Domestic Violence: Guidelines for Pastors – working with the abuser," Seattle, WA, FaithTrust Institute, www.faithtrustinstitute.org

Why Doesn't a Victim Leave?

There are several reasons why a battered woman will not leave. Some of them include:

- She loves her partner.

- She may think she alone can help him to quit battering, may believe he is sick, or a victim of forces outside himself.

- She came out of an abusive home, and may believe that a violent relationship is normal.

- She may think she is the only woman being abused, so she feels embarrassed to admit being abused.

- Her partner threatens to kill her, to kill others, and/or to kill himself if she leaves (see *How To Identify A Lethal Abuser*).

- Economics: She doubts that she can make it alone financially or that she will be able to meet her children's needs. She has no job or independent living skills; she will have no "home."

- She wants to protect the image of her partner and the family.

- Even though he abuses her, he is her only support system; he has isolated her from outside relationships.

- She is convinced that each time there is a violent episode, it will be the last.

- She does not realize she has the right not to be abused.

- She fears living alone.

- She blames herself and believes the battering will stop if she improves or stops making mistakes.

- Religious and cultural beliefs keep her in the relationship.

- She stays for the children. Any father is better than no father.

- He is not always brutal. After a violent episode, the partner often is contrite, pleads for forgiveness, and promises it will never happen again; for awhile he behaves like a model partner and father.

- She knows nothing about available services and feels trapped.

Why Does a Victim Leave?

There are also reasons why she does take the steps to leave an abusive relationship, even a marriage. These include:

- She believes another beating episode is coming, which may be fatal.

- He has begun to abuse the children.

- The children may have begun to abuse her and she realizes she must remove them from the situation.

- She has heard of available help on the radio, television, through friends or her pastor.

- She hears of other women who have left; this gives her courage to leave.

- A friend, family member, or clergy member has given her the support she needs.

How to Identify a Lethal Abuser

While not every abuser fits this profile, it is imperative that we keep the perspective that this is a life and death situation for all involved. While the factors listed below do not guarantee a lethal threat, they have been identified as "strong predictors" according to a study released by the American Journal of Public Health.[27]

- Does he have access to guns?

- Has he made threats of "deadly violence" toward his partner (i.e. threats with a weapon or to kill his victim)?

- Is he unemployed?

- Does he use illicit drugs?

- Are they in the process of separation?

- Does her partner try to control all of her daily activities?

[27] American Journal of Public Health, *Risk Factors for Femicide in Abusive Relationships: Results From a Multisite Case Control Study,* (July 2003, Vol. 93, No.7).

Frequently Asked Questions[28]

Often, when you are helping a couple through healing from issues of abuse, there are many questions you will be asked by the victim. Here are some of the most often asked questions:

If he's sorry, has he changed?

It is common for an abusive man to be apologetic after being abusive. But this doesn't mean he'll stop being violent. In fact, many batterers have a repeating cycle where there's a stage of increasing abusiveness, then an incident of violence, followed by a period of regret and attempts to make up. He may try to use the apologies and promises to get his victim to come back, to drop a restraining order, or to drop criminal charges.

This remorseful stage is just another tactic of his abuse and control of her, and does not lead to any lasting changes.

Can he really change?

Yes, but progress will depend on his recognizing his problem and being prepared to work hard on it for a long time, without expecting rewards or support from his partner for his efforts. Change does not occur overnight, if it occurs at all, and many men drop out along the way. Long term improvement in behavior is more likely for a man who completes the full-year program, but even that is no guarantee; many men continue to be violent and controlling after counseling.

Should they try couples counseling?

No. Couples counseling allows him to stay focused on his criticisms of his victim, instead of dealing with his own problem. He may even retaliate against her physically or verbally for what she says to the counselor.

The victim may also be put under pressure to give up certain things that are important to her in return for his giving up his violence. *Abuse is a problem in the abuser, not a problem in the relationship.* For these reasons, couples counseling is not helpful as an alternative to an intervention program for the abuser.

Couples counseling may be helpful in working out other problems, after he has gone a long period (at least 9 months) of using no violence or intimidation, and when he shows signs of being consistent in treating his partner better.

[28] Adapted from *Emerge* handout, Cambridge, MA 02140: Emerge, 1998.

Why an Intervention Program?

Goals of an intervention program for someone who abuses include:

- Learning to identify abusive behavior.
- Stopping all abusive behavior toward partner or children.
- Ending intimidating behavior (throwing things, standing up during arguments, threatening, giving scary looks, etc.)
- Stopping verbal abuse and criticism (name-calling, ridiculing, yelling, swearing, insulting).
- Ceasing to blame partner or children for feelings and behavior.
- Learning to recognize the effects of violence on family members.
- Learning ways to handle conflict non-abusively.
- Learning how attitudes and beliefs give permission to use abusive behavior.
- Learning to listen better.

Is he violent because he drinks?

Alcohol does not cause a man to be abusive; it just gives him a convenient excuse. If he is violent and he also abuses alcohol, then he has two problems that he has to take care of. A substance abusing batterer typically has a period of improved behavior when he first gets off the substance, and then heads rapidly back to his old abusive ways.

Although the battering and substance abuse are two separate problems, it is true that *a substance-abusing batterer is often particularly dangerous.* And he will have to get off of the substance in order to make any meaningful progress on his battering problem.

How to know if he's changing?

His partner is the best judge of whether he is changing or not; if her gut feeling is that he has not changed, trust that regardless of other signs. Some of the things to look for are:

- Has he completely stopped saying and doing things that will hurt her?
- Can she express anger toward him and not be punished for it?
- Does it feel safe to bring up topics that will upset him?
- Can he listen to her opinion and respect it even when he disagrees?
- Can he argue without being abusive or domineering?
- Does he respect her wishes about sex and physical contact?
- Has he stopped expecting her to do things for him?
- Can she spend times with friends without being afraid that he'll retaliate?
- Can she do things that are important to her, like get a job or go to school?
- Is she comfortable with the way he interacts with the children? Does she feel safe leaving them alone with him?
- Is he being supportive and giving her compliments?
- Does he listen well to her?
- Does he do his share of the housework and childcare?

Some signs that he is *not* changing include:

- Does he use what he is learning in the program against her in any way?
- Does he tell her that she is abusive?
- Is he pressuring her to go to therapy for herself or couples counseling for the two of them?
- Is he making his abuse sound a lot less severe than it really is when he talks about it?
- Does he tell her that she owes him another chance? Does he say that he can't change without her support? Does he try to get her or the children to feel sorry for him?
- Does she have to keep after him to attend his sessions and stay in the program?
- Is he pressuring her to make up her mind about the relationship or to move back in together?
- Is he pressuring her to drop criminal charges or the restraining order?

Love of Power Wheel [29]

Abusive relationships are based on the erroneous belief that one person has the right to control the actions of another. When the actions described within the spokes of this wheel prove insufficient, the person in power moves on to actual physical and sexual violence. The relationship is based on the exercise of power to gain/maintain control. The dignity of both partners is stripped away.

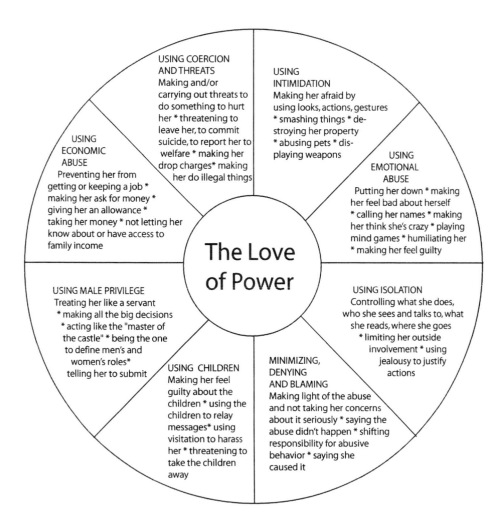

USING COERCION AND THREATS
Making and/or carrying out threats to do something to hurt her * threatening to leave her, to commit suicide, to report her to welfare * making her drop charges* making her do illegal things

USING INTIMIDATION
Making her afraid by using looks, actions, gestures * smashing things * destroying her property * abusing pets * displaying weapons

USING EMOTIONAL ABUSE
Putting her down * making her feel bad about herself * calling her names * making her think she's crazy * playing mind games * humiliating her * making her feel guilty

USING ECONOMIC ABUSE
Preventing her from getting or keeping a job * making her ask for money * giving her an allowance * taking her money * not letting her know about or have access to family income

USING MALE PRIVILEGE
Treating her like a servant * making all the big decisions * acting like the "master of the castle" * being the one to define men's and women's roles* telling her to submit

USING CHILDREN
Making her feel guilty about the children * using the children to relay messages* using visitation to harass her * threatening to take the children away

MINIMIZING, DENYING AND BLAMING
Making light of the abuse and not taking her concerns about it seriously * saying the abuse didn't happen * shifting responsibility for abusive behavior * saying she caused it

USING ISOLATION
Controlling what she does, who she sees and talks to, what she reads, where she goes * limiting her outside involvement * using jealousy to justify actions

The Love of Power

[29] Adapted from: *Domestic Abuse Intervention Project.* Duluth, MN 55802

Power of Love Wheel [30]

Healthy relationships are based on the belief that two people in a relationship are partners with equal rights to have their needs met and equal responsibility for the success of the partnership. Given this belief system, violence is not an option because it so thoroughly violates the rights of one partner and jeopardizes the success of the partnership. In a relationship based on equality, the dignity of both partners is enhanced.

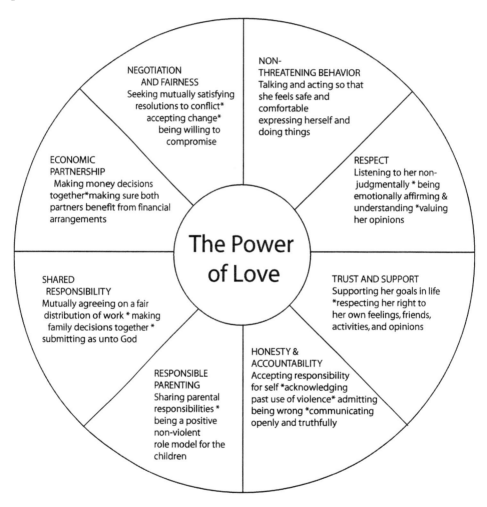

[30] Adapted from: *Domestic Abuse Intervention Project.* Duluth, MN 55802

Books and Videos for Pastors

FaithTrust Institute, *Domestic Violence: What Churches Can Do* (Video), Seattle, WA: FaithTrust Institute, 2002

Fortune, Marie M. *Keeping the Faith: Guidance for Christian Women Facing Abuse.* New York, San Francisco: Harper Collins, 1995. *(Also available in Spanish and Korean versions: www.faithtrustinstitute.org)*

Fortune, Marie M. *Violence in the Family: A Workshop Curriculum for Clergy and Other Helpers.* Cleveland, OH: The Pilgrim Press, 2002.

Horton, Anne L. and Judith A. Williams, eds. *Abuse and Religion: When Praying Isn't Enough.* Lanham, MD: Lexington Books, 1988.

Kroeger, Catherine Clark and James R. Beck, eds. *Healing the Hurting.* Grand Rapids, MI: Baker, 1998.

Kroeger, Catherine Clark and Nancy Nason-Clark. *No Place for Abuse: Biblical & Practical Resources to Counteract Domestic Violence.* Downers Grove, IL: InterVarsity Press, 2001.

Kroeger, Catherine Clark and James R. Beck, eds. *Women, Abuse, and the Bible.* Grand Rapids, MI: Baker Books, 1996.

Miles, Al. *Domestic Violence: What Every Pastor Needs to Know.* Minneapolis, MN: Fortress Press, 2000.

Miles, Al. *Violence in Families: What Every Christian Needs to Know.* Minneapolis, MN: Augsburg Fortress Publishers, 2002.

Miller, Melissa A. *Family Violence: The Compassionate Church Responds.* Scottdale, PA: Herald Press, 1994.

Monfalcone, Wesley R. *Coping With Abuse in the Family*. Louisville, KY: Westminster John Knox Press, 1980.

Nason-Clark, Nancy. *The Battered Wife: How Christians Confront Family Violence*. Louisville, KY: Westminster/John Knox Press, 1997.

Sutter, Cathy A. and Howard Green. *A Christian Response to Domestic Violence: A Reconciliation Model for Social Workers*. St. David's: North American Association of Christians in Social Work, 1985.

Switzer, M'Liss and Katherine Hale. *Called to Account*. Seattle, WA: The Seal Press, 1987.

Walters, Candace. *Invisible Wounds*. Portland, OR: Multnomah Press, 1992.

Weatherhead, Leslie D. *The Will of God*. Nashville, TN: Abingdon Press, 1991.

Faith-Based Organizations & Other Helpful Websites

Christian Recovery International
Website: www.christianrecovery.com

*Christian Recovery International is a coalition of ministries dedicated to helping the Christian community become a safe and helpful place for people recovering from addiction, abuse, or trauma.

FaithTrust Institute
2400 North 45th Street #10
Seattle, Washington 98103
Phone: 206-634-1903
Fax: 206-634-0115
Email: info@faithtrustinstitute.org
Website: www.faithtrustinstitute.org

*FaithTrust Institute, a nonprofit organization, is a multifaith resource working to end sexual and domestic violence. Through training, educational presentations, and multimedia materials, FaithTrust Institute provides religious communities and advocates with the tools and knowledge they need to address the faith aspects of abuse. Founded in 1977 by the Rev. Dr. Marie M. Fortune, FaithTrust Institute offers a wide range of services and resources, including training, consultation, and educational materials.

Family Renewal Shelter
The Rev. Keith Galbraith, Director
6832 Pacific Avenue
Tacoma, Washington 98408
Business Phone: 253-475-9010
Crisis Line: 800-550-3915
Email: staff@dvhelp.org
Website: http://www.domesticviolencehelp.org

*Since 1986 Family Renewal Shelter has offered the necessities of safety and life to domestic violence victims at highest risk. Beside these basic services, an on-site medical clinic, technology center, spiritual support, survival self-defense classes, pet therapy, animal kennel, "Cars For Families" program and educational scholarships are also provided.

Global Institute on Violence & Exploitation (G.I.V.E.)
Nancy Murphy, Co-Founder
Sig Swanstrom, Co-Founder
409 D Street NE
Washington, DC 20002
Phone: 866-362-5153
Email: nmurphy@G-I-V-E.org
Website: www.G-I-V-E.org

*The "Global Institute on Violence & Exploitation" (GIVE) brings together people, research and resources to facilitate solutions to the problems of abuse, domestic violence, sexual assault and trafficking in persons. GIVE is a hub for knowledge, and a crossroads for activity. It operates as a strategic partnership to end violence and exploitation on the streets and at home in order to facilitate safe, loving, equitable relationships and break the cycle of abuse. GIVE exists to help its members achieve greater effectiveness in stopping abuse. GIVE has many resources and samples for personal and congregational use, including Bible Study samples, resolutions, additional booklists, video resources, handouts, nationwide referrals, web resources, and more.

HOPE NOW
Dr. Randy Bridges, Ministry Director
PO Box 6
Mountlake Terrace, WA 98043-0006
Phone: 866-888-4673
Website: www.hopenow.net

* Hope Now is a not-for-profit Christian organization dedicated to providing hope and help to the hidden hurting now. Hope Now helps people transform their lives by dealing with difficult personal issues. Hope Now is an action-oriented ministry that offers resources to churches, families and individuals. Through an inter-faith alliance of religious leaders, Hope Now develops and delivers programs that are based on Biblical principles and values, and provides open solutions to hidden sin through education, healing and acceptance.

Mars Hill Graduate School
2525 220th St, Suite 100
Bothell, WA 98021
Phone: 888-977-2002
Fax: 425-806-5599
Email: info@mhgs.edu
Website: www.mhgs.edu

*Mars Hill Graduate School's mission is to train people to be competent in the study of the Scriptures, the culture, and the human soul by deepening their commitment to relationships and addressing the needs of a rapidly changing culture. MHGS offers a Certificate in Domestic Violence Advocacy to prepare leaders to meet the urgent need of providing safety for victims, accountability for perpetrators and overall prevention of domestic violence.

Northwest Family Life Learning and Counseling Center
1015 NE 113th Street
Seattle, Washington 98125
Phone: 206-363-9601
Fax: 206-363-9639
Email: hope@nwfamilylife.org
Website: www.northwestfamilylife.org

*Northwest Family Life exists to assist individuals and families find hope and healing when faced with the pain of domestic violence and related issues. Services include: Advocacy and Support for adult and child victims of domestic violence, State-Certified Domestic Violence Treatment Program, State-Certified Chemical Dependency Program, General Counseling and Spiritual Direction.

Union Gospel Mission-Olympia Branch
Website: www.ougm.org

*Offers a variety of information and resources on domestic violence, including 37 Bible studies on domestic violence issue. These studies are also suitable for use in a classroom or support group setting.

World Evangelical Alliance—
Commission on Women's Concerns
270 Elm Street
Shafter, CA 93263
Phone: 661-746-4748
Fax: 611-746-3035
Email: ewbartel@lightspeed.net
Website: http://www.worldevangelical.org/cwc.html

*This Commission exists to meet the unique needs of women around the world. In doing so, the CWC provides an internationally respected voice for women, especially in the church. It identifies concerns and solutions, and calls the church and the evangelical community to give more public attention to the plight of women, to recognize all injustices women experience, and to take action to alleviate them. The CWC also calls the church and the evangelical community together for networking, facilitating, mobilizing, motivating and cooperating as a global body in the area of women's concerns.

Questions for Women to Answer to Reveal Domestic Abuse

Physical violence is only one aspect of abuse. Here are several additional indicators that highlight abusive behavior. If a woman answers "yes" to several of these questions, she may be at risk:

- Is there blaming, cursing, or name calling?

- Does one person control the finances?

- Does your partner control your outside activities, interests, and friendships?

- Do you notice a dual personality in your partner?

- Do you make excuses for your partner's behavior?

- Do you feel pressured to have sex with your partner when you don't want to?

- Were the parents of either you or your partner abusive?

- Does your partner play mind games, use hostile humor, put downs, or ignore or belittle you in public?

- Are you afraid to express your own opinion?

- Do you feel the household responsibilities are not shared?

- Are you having trouble communicating?

- Do you live in fear of your partner?

- Do you have any unrealistic expectations of yourself or others?

- Is there isolation from friends and/or family?

- Does one person make all the decisions?

- Are there threats or intimidation by looks, actions, or voice?

- Is there undue jealousy of friends, family, and time?

- Is there destruction of personal property?

- Are your children being used as pawns?

- Have you noticed a change in your self-esteem?

- Does your partner have explosions, and then bring you flowers, gifts, etc?

- Does he promise to change his behavior, and then the cycle starts all over again?

Books and Videos for Use with Abused Women

Allender, Dr. Dan B. and Dr. Tremper Longman III. *Bold Love.* Colorado Springs, CO: Navpress, 1993.

Allender, Dr. Dan B. *The Healing Path: How the Hurts in Your Past Can Lead You to a More Abundant Life.* Colorado Springs, CO: Waterbrook Press, 2000.

Allender, Dr. Dan B. and Dr. Tremper Longman III. *Intimate Allies.* Carol Stream, IL: Tyndale House, 1999.

Allender, Dr. Dan B. *The Wounded Heart: Hope for Adult Victims of Childhood Sexual Abuse.* Colorado Springs, CO: Navpress, 1990.

Alsdurf, James and Phyllis Alsdurf. *Battered into Submission: The Tragedy of Wife Abuse in the Christian Home.* Downers Grove, IL: InterVaristy Press, 1989.

Bhuler, Rich. *Pain and Pretending: You Can Be Set Free From the Hurts of the Past.* Nashville, TN: Thomas Nelson, Inc, 1988.

Blue, Ken. *Healing Spiritual Abuse.* Downer's Grove, IL: InterVarsity Press, 1993.

De Becker, Gavin. *The Gift of Fear.* New York: Little Brown & Co., 1997.

Dutton, Donald. *The Batterer.* New York: Basic Books, 1995.

Evans, Patricia. *The Verbally Abusive Relationship: How to Recognize It and How to Respond.* Holbrock, MA: Adams Media Corporation, 1996.

Ezell, Lee. *The Missing Piece.* Ann Arbor, MI: Servant Publications, 1992.

FaithTrust Institute. *Wings Like a Dove: Healing for the Abused Christian Woman (Video).* Seattle, WA: FaithTrust Institute, 1997.

Fortune, Marie M. *Keeping the Faith: Guidance for Christian Women Facing Abuse.* New York, San Francisco: Harper Collins, 1995. *(Also available in Spanish and Korean versions: www.faithtrustinstitute.org)*

Gondolf, Edward. *Man Against Woman: What Every Woman Should Know About Violent Men.* Blue Ridge Summit, PA: TAB Books, 1989.

Herman, Judith Lewis. *Trauma and Recovery.* New York: Basic Books, 1992.

Horton, Anne L. and Judith A. Williams, eds. *Abuse and Religion: When Praying Isn't Enough*. Lanham, MD: Lexington Books, 1988.

Ketterman, Grace. *Verbal Abuse*. Ann Arbor, MI: Servant Publications, 1992.

Jackson, Tim and Jeff Olson. *Discovery Series: When Violence Comes Home*. Grand Rapids, MI: Radio Bible Class, 1995.

Jackson, Tim. *Discovery Series: When Anger Burns*. Grand Rapids, MI: Radio Bible Class, 1994.

Jacobson, Neil and John Gottman. *When Men Batter Women: New Insights into Ending Abusive Relationships*. New York: Simon and Schuster, 1998.

Jones, Ann and Susan Schechter. *When Loves Goes Wrong: What to do When You Can't Do Anything Right: Strategies for Women With Controlling Partners*, New York: HarperCollins, 1992.

Kroeger, Catherine Clark and James R. Beck, eds. *Healing the Hurting*. Grand Rapids, MI: Baker Books, 1998.

Kroeger, Catherine Clark and Nancy Nason-Clark. *No Place for Abuse: Biblical & Practical Resources to Counteract Domestic Violence*. Downers Grove, IL: InterVarsity Press, 2001.

Kroeger, Catherine Clark and James R. Beck, eds. *Women, Abuse, and the Bible*. Grand Rapids, MI: Baker, 1996.

Levison, David. *Family Violence in Cross Cultural Perspectives*. Thousand Oaks, CA: Sage Publications, 1989.

Means, Marsha. *Living With Your Husband's Secret Wars*. Grand Rapids, MI: Baker Books, 1999.

Nason-Clark, Nancy. *The Battered Wife: How Christians Confront Family Violence*. Louisville, KY: Westminster/John Knox Press, 1997.

NiCarthy, Ginny. *You Can Be Free: An Easy-to-Read Handbook for Abused Women*. Seattle, WA: Seal Press.

Strom, Kay Marshall. *In the Name of Submission*. Portland, OR: Multnomah Press, 1986.

Twerski, Abraham. *The Shame Borne in Silence: Spouse Abuse in the Jewish Community*. Pittsburgh, PA: Mirkov Publications, 1996.

Walker, Lenore. *The Battered Woman*. New York: Harper and Row, 1979.

White, Evelyn. *Chain, Chain, Change: For Black Women Dealing with Physical and Emotional Abuse*. Seattle, WA: Seal Press, 1985.

Zambrano, Myrna. *Mejor Sola Que Mal Acompañada: Para la Mujer Golpeada/ For the Latina in an Abusive Relationship*. Seattle, WA: Seal Press, 1985.

Books for Use with Abusers

Allender, Dr. Dan B. and Dr. Tremper Longman III. *Bold Love.* Colorado Springs: Navpress, 1993.

Allender, Dr. Dan B. and Dr. Tremper Longman III. *Intimate Allies.* Carol Stream, IL: Tyndale House Publishers, 1999.

Brod, Harry. *A Mensch Among Men: Explorations in Jewish Masculinity.* Freedom, CA: The Crossing Press, 1988.

Dutton, Donald. *The Batterer.* New York: Basic Books, 1995.

Kivel, Paul. *Men's Work: How To Stop the Violence that Tears Our Lives Apart.* New York: Ballentine Books, 1992.

Klaver, Dick Brian. *Men at Peace: Solutions for Men Caught in the Cycles of Rage and Depression.* Nashville: Thomas Nelson Inc, 1993

Means, Patrick. *Men's Secret Wars.* Grand Rapids, MI: Baker Books, 1996.

Miedzian, Myriam. *Boys Will Be Boys: Breaking the Link Between Masculinity and Violence.* New York: Doubleday, 1991.

Nouwen, Henri J.M. *The Return of the Prodigal Son.* New York: DoubleDay, 1992.

Paymar, Michael. *Violent No More: Helping Men End Domestic Abuse.* Alameda: Hunter House, 1993.

Thorne-Finch, Ron. *Ending the Silence: The Origins and Treatment of Male Violence Against Women.* Toronto: University of Toronto Press, 1992.

Books for Use with Children, Teens, and Parents

Allender, Dr. Dan B. *How Children Raise Parents: The Art of Listening to Your Family*. Colorado Springs, CO: Waterbrook Press, 2003.

Davis, Diane. *Something Is Wrong at My House: A Book About Parent's Fighting*. Seattle, WA: Parenting Press, 1984.

Garbarino, James, Edna Guttman and Janis Wilson Seeley. *The Psychologically Battered Child*. San Francisco, CA: Jossey-Bass Publishers, 1986.

Garbarino, James and Gwen Gilliam. *Understanding Abusive Families*. Toronto, Canada: Lexington Books, 1980.

Johnson, Scott. *When "I Love You" Turns Violent: Emotional and Physical Abuse in Dating Relationships*. Far Hills, NJ: New Horizon Press, 1993.

Levy, Barrie, ed., *Dating Violence: Young Women in Danger*. Seattle, WA: Seal Press, 1993.

Levy, Barrie. *In Love and In Danger: A Teen's Guide to Breaking Free of Abusive Relationships*. Seattle, WA: Seal Press, 1993.

McDermott, Judith and Frances Wells Burck. *Children of Domestic Violence: A Guide for Moms*. Rockland Family Shelter, 1990.

Paris, Susan. *Mommy and Daddy Are Fighting*. Seattle, WA: Parenting Press, 1986.

Rue, Nancy. *Coping with Date Violence*. New York: Rosen Publishing Group, 1989.

We Can't Play at My House: Children and Family Violence, Book 1: Handbook for Parents. Boulder, CO: Boulder County Safehouse, 1990.

We Can't Play at My House: Children and Family Violence, Book 2: Handbook for Teachers. Boulder, CO: Boulder County Safehouse, 1990.

Nancy Murphy is the Executive Director of Northwest Family Life Learning and Counseling Center, a Seattle-based non-profit agency dedicated to assisting individuals and families find hope and healing when facing the pain of domestic violence. NWFL offers advocacy and support for abused women and children as well as a state-certified intervention program for batterers. Nancy's primary responsibilities include community education and speaking engagements. She is a frequent guest on radio programs focused on issues of violence, anger, and trauma. She also provides training for professionals around the globe and has had the opportunity to address several international audiences.

Raised in a missionary home on the west coast of Vancouver Island, Nancy grew up with a strong faith in the Lord. She began her scholastic career at Trinity Western College in British Columbia. She finished her Bachelor's degree in Anthropology and Social Service at Seattle Pacific University and went on to complete a Master's of Applied Behavioral Science at City University, with a major in Counseling. She is a licensed mental health counselor in the state of Washington and a nationally certified counselor.

Presently, Nancy is working on her D. Min. in Transformational Leadership through Northwest Graduate School. She serves on the Board of the Faith Based Network as well as the Women's Leadership Forum. She is the Co-Founder and President of the Global Initiative on Violence and Exploitation (GIVE). She is a Clinical Professor at Mars Hill Graduate School, where she directs the Certificate in Domestic Violence Advocacy program. Nancy has the support and encouragement of her husband, Tom Murphy, and their five children.